Caribbean Cooking

RECIPES, LANDSCAPES & PEOPLE

Camilla de la Bédoyère   General Editor: **Gina Steer**

STAR FIRE

Contents

Introduction

Picture ivory-white sandy beaches, palm trees dipping their fronds into crystalline turquoise waters and sailboats lazily drifting to shore – and you will be conjuring up a Caribbean paradise. Yet it is the sight, aroma and taste sensations of well-prepared food that are most evocative of times and places, and revitalize memories in a way that photographs can never recapture.

Whether the Caribbean is familiar to you or not, you can explore the region's culinary delights and begin to uncover the many pleasures of Caribbean food through these pages. The story of Caribbean food, however, is not a simple one. Like the islands themselves, the peoples of the Caribbean are united in the tangled web of their combined histories. Their cultures of dance, art, music and cuisine all reflect a complex heritage that owes a debt to the present-day inhabitants and their forebears, who often faced great adversity and times of hardship.

The early inhabitants of the islands – Amerindians and Caribs – brought food and recipes from the Americas. When Christopher Columbus toured the region in the late fifteenth century, his Spanish forces were the vanguard of a huge European movement that wanted to colonize the Caribbean, and exploit its rich reserves of natural resources. The European powers battled for centuries over the various territories, each wanting to increase its hold in the region. They caused turmoil, instability and loss of life while doing so. Islands were passed between French, British, Spanish, Dutch and Portuguese hands following many bloody battles.

African slaves, mostly from the Gold Coast, were shipped to the islands in their thousands to work the sugar plantations, and migrants from Asia came to seek their fortunes in prospering economies. With each wave of immigration came new ingredients, ideas and inspiration – and recipes gradually evolved, usually passed from mother to daughter by word of mouth. Now, a single Caribbean menu may display this rich tapestry of cuisine with listings of Creole jerk chicken, Indian curried goat and an Indonesian rice table. The variety of dishes on offer certainly gives a fascinating insight into the region's unsettled history.

Fruits of the Soil

Not all Caribbean islands are fertile, but most of them can be cultivated to some degree. Enjoying a tropical climate, the region benefits from both sunshine and rain, and many islands are verdant, lush places where mango and papaya trees line the earthen tracks and tarmac roads. It is not unusual to see mango trees so laden with ripe fruits that the mangoes fall to the ground before anyone – except the enthralled tourist – notices them. Sugar cane was once the dominant crop on many islands; it is still grown extensively (and used not just to produce sugar, but molasses and rum, too). Pineapples are native to Jamaica, and these tropical fruits were sent to Hawaii – but other plants were introduced to the region from elsewhere, and have become firmly established in both the soil and the cuisine. Bananas, Bombay mangoes, and citrus trees are all immigrants; the popular breadfruit was introduced to Jamaica by Captain Bligh, of mutiny fame. Okra, an important plant in Caribbean cooking, was imported by African slaves and is used as a vegetable and a thickener.

Fruits of the Sea

Visitors to the Caribbean naturally gravitate to the coast, where beautiful vistas can be enjoyed from a beachside tavern or restaurant, while sampling the fruits of the sea. Fish and shellfish, of course, play an important role in Caribbean cuisine. The clear waters of the Caribbean Sea and Atlantic Ocean offer a range of delights to the fish chef; from sea urchins, conch and octopus to grouper, snapper and marlin. Fish soups and chowders are common throughout the Caribbean; with a smattering of locally grown vegetables and the addition of herbs and spices, each island produces a unique version.

As with all nations that rely heavily on fish and shellfish for protein, Caribbean islanders are increasingly aware of the problems of over-fishing. Fishing seasons are being established in some areas to protect fish, turtle and conch stocks, and the resourceful Caribbean islanders are substituting some common species for those that are in decline. Fish recipes generally can be easily adapted to suit the fish that is available to the cook.

Spices & Seasonings

Caribbean food is rarely bland in colour or flavour. The simple food staples of African slaves were turned into lively meals by the addition of spices, borrowing ideas from the Spanish, French, Indians and Chinese. Starchy root vegetables such as cassava or potato are spiced up with a splash of hot pepper sauce or sprinkling of cayenne. The most famous of all Caribbean seasonings, however, is Jamaican jerk. The fiery, spicy mixture contains allspice and Scotch bonnet peppers, which are among the hottest available. Cloves, cinnamon, garlic, nutmeg and thyme are some of the other ingredients added to the blend. The paste is rubbed into the meat before cooking, ideally over wood or charcoal.

Pleasure is an integral part of the Caribbean way of life. Hassle, hustle and haste simply don't feature; enjoyment of food is part and parcel of this laconic, laid-back lifestyle. Islanders may be aware that fried treats from street vendors, such as fritters, are not the healthiest of foods, but they take the view that all things are fine in moderation – and get on with enjoying the sensations of taste and smell.

Many Caribbean recipes may appear complex because of the numbers of spices or herbs involved, but in reality they can all be prepared at a leisurely pace, and stews and soups often benefit from long, gentle cooking; frenetically prepared food is not the Caribbean approach. Gentle stewing allows flavours from the seasoning to infuse, and the cook can add a little more from time to time, until the meat reaches a point of perfect succulence. The cooking pot, rather like the Caribbean itself, benefits from a heady mix of different ingredients, which come together over time, to blend into something entirely new and wonderful.

oa & Jamaica

Lying at the north and west of the Caribbean, the Bahamas, Cuba and Jamaica show the huge range of cultural influences that typifies the cuisine of the region.

The Bahamas

The Bahamas are a large group of more than 700 islands and tiny coral cays, stretching in an archipelago over 100,000 square miles (260,000 square kilometres) in the Atlantic Ocean. The inhabited islands have an exceptionally strong European and American influence, due in part to their close proximity to Florida. Despite problems associated with poverty (like most of the Caribbean), the Bahamas are among the wealthiest of all the Caribbean islands, with an income derived from a healthy tourist trade and a flourishing financial services industry.

The islands came under British rule in 1718, and remained relatively stable politically from there on, gaining full independence from Britain in 1973. Their food, however, is truly international, with worldwide influences. While some foods are treated with a delicate touch, others are doused in fiery pepper sauces – for the cuisine of the Bahamas has been greatly influenced by the American South.

Local seafood is a staple, being plentiful in the turquoise crystal-clear waters that surround the islands. Dishes with crayfish are a fine example of Bahamian cuisine. Crayfish are small, spiny crustaceans (also known as rock lobsters) which are served minced, boiled or added to salads. Conch (pronounced 'konk') is a shellfish with firm, tasty meat that is often added to chowders, or sprinkled with lime juice and spices before frying, making a popular bite-sized bar snack. Land crabs can be seen scuttling across roads at dusk, and are particularly delicious boiled or baked. Locally available fish include red snapper, yellowtail and grouper, which is boiled to maintain its delicate flavour and flaky texture. Rice or grits are often served with fish and crab dishes, with macaroni and cheese, or potato salad. The islands are strewn with coconut trees, and coconut milk and flesh are used liberally in many recipes.

Cuba

Few islands in the Caribbean evoke the complex atmosphere of Latin American excitement, exuberance and sheer hardship as vividly as Cuba. With its traumatic history and politics, this island, the largest of the Greater Antilles, has captivated and fascinated writers such as Ernest Hemingway and Pedro Juan Gutiérrez, and inspired artists such as Jean-Baptiste Vermay. Cubans have an extraordinary ability to survive; in the recent past the island has been the stage for corruption, communist revolution, crime waves and great poverty. Nevertheless, the resilient people are able to lay their worries to one side and celebrate life with carnival, great food, music and dance, such as the rumba, cha cha, salsa and danzón.

The Cubans are less enamoured of the spicy chillies and curries found in such abundance elsewhere in the Caribbean. Like those of neighbouring islands, Cuba's cultural heritage is a mixture of influences, which all contribute flavours, colours and textures to the nation's cuisine. African, Arabic, Portuguese, Spanish, Creole and Chinese immigrants have all added to Cuban food. For historical reasons, however, there is considerable regionality in the traditional cuisine. *Comida criolla* (Creole cooking), for example, is found mostly in the east.

The main ingredient for most traditional dishes is a sauté of green peppers, onions, garlic and bay leaves, called *sofrito*, and olive oil is liberally used to cook meat, poultry, fish and vegetables. Dishes are rarely deep-fried; sautéing and slow cooking are the preferred methods, allowing cooks to be more leisurely in the kitchen and to continually adjust the seasoning until the point of perfection is reached. Cuban meat dishes, in particular, are famous for their marinades and slow cooking, which combine to produce melt-in-the-mouth tenderness.

Jamaica

The huge depth and variety of Jamaica's culinary delights owes much to the size of the island. For this is the third-largest Caribbean island and, with an area of more than 1,500 square kilometres, it is one of the few islands that is able to sustain agriculture on a commercial level.

The islanders are less dependent on imported food than many of their neighbours, and have become experts at using local produce to create a rich and diverse range of dishes. There are some large-scale orchards on the island, but it is the smaller farmers who dominate the agricultural landscape, producing mixed crops of colourful fruit and vegetables, such as mangoes, bananas, limes, avocados and sugar cane. In the cooler mountain region, green crops of lettuce, cabbage, pak choi, spring onions and herbs do

well. While many of the crops are indigenous, the huge range owes much to the efforts of immigrants who have, over centuries, introduced new varieties of plants to the island.

The cultural roots of Jamaica are steeped in a complex history that has seen the integration of many peoples, including Amerindians, African slaves and colonizing Europeans. Each new wave of immigration has brought fresh ideas to the cooking pot. The result is a heady, vibrant and exciting blend of tangy tropical fruit, burning chillies and spicy curries. Spicy goat curries, sweet and sour pork, salted cod, stewed peas and jerked meat might be accompanied by carbohydrate-rich foods such as rice, yams and cassava. Banana loaf, banana fritters, tropical fruit salad and coconut ice cream are all perfect ways to finish off a traditional Jamaican meal. With such a wonderful array of flavours and colours to tempt the palate, it is no surprise that visitors to Jamaica return home enthused and inspired to re-create their favourite dishes in their own kitchens.

Caribbean

Cooking
Snacks

Caribbean islanders love to eat on the move, and buying snacks from roadside vendors is a delightful, delicious and cheap way to enjoy local cuisine.

As in many parts of Africa, Caribbean street food is part of the everyday diet of most families, so it needs to be nutritionally balanced and is often packed with the energy-giving goodness of complex carbohydrates.

Fritters made from conch, salt cod or corn are a perennial favourite and are usually offered with spicy accompaniments to excite the palate. Satay sticks and crispy sweet potato crisps with a mango salsa are perfect appetizers, and easy to prepare at home.

Sweet Potato Crisps with Mango Salsa

These delicious crisps make an even tastier snack when served with the salsa. Why not try them with a glass or two of rum punch.

To make the salsa, mix the mango with the tomato, cucumber and onion. Add the sugar, chilli, vinegar, oil and lime zest and juice. Mix together thoroughly, cover with clingfilm and leave for 45–50 minutes.

Soak the sweet potato in cold water for 40 minutes to remove as much of the excess starch as possible. Drain and dry thoroughly on a clean tea towel or absorbent kitchen paper.

Heat the vegetable oil to 190°C/375°F in a deep-fryer. When at the correct temperature, place half the potato in the frying basket, then carefully lower the potato into the hot oil and cook for 4–5 minutes or until golden brown, shaking the basket every minute so that the potato does not stick together.

Drain the potato crisps on absorbent kitchen paper. Spread out in a single layer on a grill tray or baking sheet, sprinkle with sea salt and place under a preheated moderate grill for a few seconds to dry out. Repeat the process with the remaining potato.

Stir the mint into the salsa and serve with the potato crisps.

INGREDIENTS   Serves 6

For the Salsa

- **1 large mango, peeled, stoned and cut into small cubes**
- **8 cherry tomatoes, quartered**
- **$^1/_2$ cucumber, peeled if preferred and finely diced**
- **1 red onion, peeled and finely chopped**
- **pinch of sugar**
- **1 red chilli, deseeded and finely chopped**
- **2 tbsp white wine vinegar**
- **2 tbsp olive oil**
- **grated zest and juice of 1 lime**
- **2 tbsp freshly chopped mint**
- **450 g/1 lb sweet potatoes, peeled and thinly sliced**
- **vegetable oil for deep-frying**
- **sea salt**

HELPFUL HINT

Take care when deep-frying. Use a deep heavy-based saucepan or purpose-made deep-fryer, and fill the pan no more than one-third with oil. If you do not have a food thermometer to check the temperature, drop a cube of bread into the oil. At the correct heat, it will turn golden brown in 40 seconds.

Sweet Potato Cakes with Mango & Tomato Salsa

Sweet potatoes are used extensively in the Caribbean. There are two varieties: white sweet potato, also known as boniato, and the more common yellow variety. They can be boiled, mashed, baked or fried.

Steam or cook the sweet potato in lightly salted boiling water for 15–20 minutes until tender. Drain well, then mash until smooth.

Melt the butter in a saucepan. Add the onion and garlic, and cook gently for 10 minutes until soft. Add to the mashed sweet potato and season with the nutmeg, allspice, salt and pepper. Stir together until mixed thoroughly. Leave to cool.

Shape the mixture into 4 oval potato cakes, about 2.5 cm/1 inch thick. Dip first in the beaten egg, allowing the excess to fall back into the bowl, then coat in the polenta. Refrigerate for at least 30 minutes.

Meanwhile, mix together all the ingredients for the salsa. Spoon into a serving bowl, cover with clingfilm and leave at room temperature to allow the flavours to develop.

Heat the oil in a frying pan and cook the potato cakes for 4–5 minutes on each side. Serve with the salsa and salad leaves.

HELPFUL HINT

As an alternative to Polenta, fresh breadcrumbs can be used (or you could even use dried ones).

INGREDIENTS   Serves 4

- **700 g/1 ¹/₂ lb sweet potatoes, peeled and cut into large chunks**
- **25 g/1 oz butter**
- **1 onion, peeled and chopped**
- **1 garlic clove, peeled and crushed**
- **pinch of freshly grated nutmeg**
- **1 tsp ground allspice**
- **1 medium egg, beaten**
- **50 g/2 oz quick-cook polenta**
- **2 tbsp vegetable oil**
- **salt and freshly ground black pepper**
- **salad leaves, to serve**

For the Salsa

- **1 ripe mango, peeled, stoned and diced**
- **6 cherry tomatoes, cut into wedges**
- **4 spring onions, trimmed and thinly sliced**
- **1 hot chilli, deseeded and finely chopped**
- **finely grated zest and juice of ¹/₂ lime**
- **2 tbsp freshly chopped mint**
- **1 tsp clear honey**

Mixed Satay Sticks

An extensive coastline means that, all kinds of seafood is enjoyed on the different islands and is cooked in many diverse ways. Here large king prawns and strips of beef steak are marinated, skewered, grilled and served with a delicious satay sauce.

Preheat the grill to high just before required. Soak 8 bamboo skewers in cold water for at least 30 minutes. Peel the prawns, leaving the tails on. Using a sharp knife, remove the black vein along the back of the prawns. Cut the beef into 1 cm/½ inch wide strips. Place the prawns and beef in separate bowls, and sprinkle each with ½ tablespoon of the lime juice.

Mix together the garlic, salt, sugar, allspice cinnamon, turmeric and vegetable oil to make a paste. Lightly brush over the prawns and beef. Cover and place in the refrigerator to marinate for at least 30 minutes, but for longer if possible.

Meanwhile, make the sauce. Pour 125 ml/4 fl oz water into a small saucepan, add the shallot and sugar, and heat gently until the sugar has dissolved. Stir in the creamed coconut and chilli powder. When melted, remove from the heat and stir in the soy sauce and peanut butter. Leave to cool slightly, then spoon into a serving dish.

Thread 3 prawns onto each of 4 skewers and divide the sliced beef between the remaining skewers.

Cook the skewers under the preheated grill for 4–5 minutes, turning occasionally. The prawns should be opaque and pink, and the beef browned on the outside, but still pink in the centre. Transfer to warmed individual serving plates, garnish with a few fresh coriander leaves and serve immediately with the warm peanut sauce.

INGREDIENTS   Serves 4

- **12 large raw prawns**
- **350 g/12 oz beef rump steak**
- **1 tbsp lime juice**
- **1 garlic clove, peeled and crushed**
- **pinch of salt**
- **2 tsp soft dark brown sugar**
- **1 tsp ground allspice**
- **1 tsp ground cinnamon**
- **¼ tsp ground turmeric**
- **1 tbsp vegetable oil**
- **fresh coriander leaves, to garnish**

Spicy Peanut Sauce

- **1 shallot, peeled and very finely chopped**
- **1 tsp demerara sugar**
- **50 g/2 oz creamed coconut, chopped**
- **pinch of chilli powder**
- **1 tbsp dark soy sauce**
- **125 g/4 oz crunchy peanut butter**

ou de Girofle
Clove

Romarin
Rosemary

Poivre-Rose
Pink-Pepper

Coriandre
Coriander

Blanc
esame

THYM

Caribbean Rice Cakes with Mango Salsa

This is a new take on a traditional recipe once made extensively throughout the islands. Evaporated milk was used, and the rice cakes were shaped into bars before being deep-fried.

Wash the rice in several changes of water until the water stays relatively clear. Drain, place in a saucepan with a tight-fitting lid and add the coconut milk, lemon grass and lime zest. Bring to the boil, cover and cook over the lowest possible heat for 10 minutes. Turn off the heat and leave to stand for 10 minutes, without lifting the lid.

Heat the wok, then add the 1 tablespoon oil and, when hot, add the garlic, ginger, red pepper and chilli. Stir-fry for 1–2 minutes until just softened, then place in a large bowl.

When the rice is ready, turn into the mixing bowl and add the egg. Season to taste with salt and pepper and mix together well. Put the breadcrumbs into a shallow dish. Form the rice mixture into 8 cakes and coat them in the breadcrumbs. Chill the rice cakes in the refrigerator for 30 minutes.

Meanwhile, make the mango salsa by mixing together all the salsa ingredients in a bowl. Reserve.

Fill a clean wok about one-third full of vegetable oil. Heat to 190°C/375°F, or until a cube of bread browns in 30 seconds. Cook the rice cakes, 1 or 2 at a time, for 2–3 minutes until golden and crisp. Drain on absorbent kitchen paper. Serve with the mango salsa.

INGREDIENTS   Serves 4

- **225 g/8 oz basmati rice**
- **400 g/14 oz can coconut milk**
- **1 lemon-grass stalk, bruised**
- **1 tbsp finely grated lime zest**
- **1 tbsp vegetable oil,
  plus extra for deep-frying**
- **1 garlic clove, peeled
  and finely chopped**
- **1 tsp freshly grated root ginger**
- **1 red pepper, deseeded
  and finely chopped**
- **1 hot chilli, deseeded
  and finely chopped**
- **1 medium egg, beaten**
- **25 g/1 oz dried breadcrumbs**

For the Salsa
- **1 large mango, peeled,
  stoned and finely chopped**
- **1 small red onion,
  peeled and finely chopped**
- **2 tbsp freshly chopped coriander**
- **2 tbsp freshly chopped basil**
- **1 hot chilli, deseeded
  and finely chopped**
- **juice of 1 lime**

Cassava Chips

Cassava is a large starchy tuber and is used extensively in Caribbean cooking. Cassava chips are perfect to serve with cocktails.

Peel the cassava and cut into thick chips about 2.5 cm/ 1 inch thick. Leave the chips in cold water while preparing the rest of the cassava to prevent discoloration.

Drain the cassava chips and place in a saucepan with the ½ teaspoon salt. Cover with cold water and bring to the boil. Reduce the heat to a simmer, cover with a lid and cook for 20–25 minutes, or until just tender. Drain, pat dry and reserve.

Heat the oil in a deep-fryer to a temperature of 190°C/375°F. Meanwhile, have ready some kitchen paper, the sea salt and ground black pepper (or the jerk seasoning), and the shredded coconut.

When the oil has reached the correct temperature, place a layer of cassava chips in the frying basket and lower into the hot oil. Cook for 5 minutes, or until crisp and golden. Drain on kitchen paper and sprinkle with either the salt and pepper or the jerk seasoning. Sprinkle with the coconut. Repeat until all the chips are cooked. Serve warm.

INGREDIENTS   Serves 4

- **450 g/1 lb cassava**
- **½ tsp salt**
- **600 ml/ 1 pt vegetable oil for deep-frying**
- **sea salt and freshly ground black pepper or 1 tsp jerk seasoning**
- **2 tbsp finely shredded coconut**

HELPFUL HINT

If preferred, cook the cassava chips in a large frying pan a few at a time. Use 3–4 tablespoons oil. For a crisper chip, freeze the blanched cassava for 1 hour before frying frozen.

Plantain Appetizer

Plantains are a member of the banana family and need cooking before eating. The flesh is ivory or yellow, or may even have a pink tinge. Plantains are best used when the skins have turned yellow. They have a high starch content, but unlike bananas are not sweet.

Peel one of the green plantains and cut into wafer-thin rounds, preferably using a swivel-headed potato peeler.

Heat 1 tablespoon of the oil in a large frying pan and fry the plantain slices for 2–3 minutes until golden, turning occasionally. Transfer to a plate lined with kitchen paper and keep warm.

Coarsely grate the other green plantain and mix with the onion.

Heat 1 tablespoon of the remaining oil in the pan and fry the plantain and onion mixture for 2–3 minutes until golden, turning occasionally. Transfer to the plate with the plantain slices.

Peel the yellow plantain and cut into small chunks. Sprinkle with cayenne pepper. Heat the remaining oil and fry the yellow plantain and garlic for 4–5 minutes until brown. Drain and sprinkle with salt.

Arrange all the plantain mixtures in a warm serving dish.

INGREDIENTS   Serves 4

- **2 green plantains**
- **3 tbsp vegetable oil**
- **1 small onion, very thinly sliced**
- **1 yellow plantain**
- **½ garlic clove, crushed**
- **cayenne pepper, for sprinkling**
- **salt, for sprinkling**

Corn Fritters with Hot & Spicy Relish

Whichever Caribbean home or restaurant you visit, you will be sure to find sweetcorn on the menu, either in a sauce, corn bread or fritters, or simply as a vegetable, added to stews, curries or gumbos. Here sweetcorn kernels have been used to make fritters which are served with a hot, spicy relish.

First make the relish. Heat a wok, add the vegetable oil and, when hot, add the onion and stir-fry for 3–4 minutes, or until softened. Add the chilli and garlic, stir-fry for 1 minute, then leave to cool slightly. Stir in the lime juice, transfer to a food processor and blend until the consistency of chutney. Reserve.

Put the sweetcorn in a food processor and blend briefly until just mashed. Transfer to a bowl with the onions, chilli powder, allspice, flour, baking powder and egg. Season to taste with salt and pepper, and mix together to form a batter.

Heat a wok, add the oil and heat to 180°C/350°F. Working in batches, drop a few spoonfuls of the sweetcorn batter into the oil and deep-fry for 3–4 minutes, until golden and crispy, turning occasionally. Using a slotted spoon, remove the fritters and drain on absorbent kitchen paper. Arrange on a warmed serving platter, garnish with sprigs of coriander and serve immediately, accompanied by the relish.

INGREDIENTS Makes 16–20

For the Spicy Relish
- **3 tbsp vegetable oil**
- **1 onion, peeled and very finely chopped**
- **¼ tsp dried crushed chillies**
- **2 garlic cloves, peeled and crushed**
- **2 tbsp lime juice**

- **325 g/11 oz can sweetcorn kernels, drained**
- **1 onion, peeled and very finely chopped**
- **1 spring onion, trimmed and very finely chopped**
- **½ tsp hot chilli powder**
- **1 tsp ground allspice**
- **4 tbsp plain flour**
- **1 tsp baking powder**
- **1 medium egg**
- **300 ml/10 fl oz vegetable oil**
- **salt and freshly ground black pepper**
- **sprigs of fresh coriander, to garnish**

Cream of Pumpkin Soup

Pumpkins are readily available throughout the islands, as are other delicious squash. This type of soup is often served in the empty shell of the same squash that is used to make it.

Cut the pumpkin flesh into 2.5 cm/1 inch cubes. Heat the olive oil in a large saucepan and cook the pumpkin for 2–3 minutes, coating it completely with the oil.

Add the onion, leek, carrot and celery to the saucepan with the garlic and chilli. Cook, stirring, for 5 minutes, or until the vegetables have begun to soften. Cover the vegetables with 1.7 litres/3 pints water and bring to the boil. Season with plenty of salt and pepper, the allspice and nutmeg. Cover and simmer for 15–20 minutes or until all the vegetables are tender.

Remove from the heat, cool slightly, then pour into a food processor or blender. Liquidize to form a smooth purée, then pass through a sieve into a clean saucepan.

Adjust the seasoning to taste and add all but 2 tablespoons of the coconut milk and enough water to obtain a thick and creamy consistency. Bring the soup to boiling point, add the cayenne pepper and serve immediately swirled with the remaining coconut milk and accompanied by warm herby bread.

INGREDIENTS   Serves 4

- **900 g/2 lb pumpkin flesh (after peeling and discarding the seeds)**
- **4 tbsp olive oil**
- **1 large onion, peeled and finely chopped**
- **1 leek, trimmed and finely chopped**
- **1 carrot, peeled and cut into small dice**
- **2 celery sticks, cut into small dice**
- **4 garlic cloves, peeled and crushed**
- **1 habañero chilli, deseeded and finely chopped**
- **1 tsp ground allspice**
- **$^{1}/_{4}$ tsp freshly grated nutmeg**
- **150 ml/5 fl oz pint coconut milk**
- **$^{1}/_{4}$ tsp cayenne pepper**
- **salt and freshly ground black pepper**
- **warm herby bread, to serve**

Further Exploring the
Gre

ater Antilles

The islands featured here, all part of the Greater Antilles, mostly have strong Spanish or Latin American roots in their culture and cuisine.

Hispaniola

One of the region's most beautiful and culturally rich islands, Hispaniola has had a chequered past. Its name, derived from *La Isla Española*, which means the Spanish Island, bears testament to the conquering powers of the Spanish in the fifteenth and sixteenth centuries, when they held sway over much of the Caribbean region. Hispaniola was first brought to the attention of Europeans by Christopher Columbus, who visited the island four times and, enraptured by the turquoise seas, majestic mountainous regions and beaches of golden sand, declared: 'There is no more beautiful island in the world.'

The indigenous Amerindians lived on the island for around 5,000 years; their ethnic roots were probably both Central and South American. A peaceful people, the Taíno Amerindians were virtually annihilated by the beginning of the seventeenth century, as the Spanish, who killed with impunity, and bearing diseases to which the Indians had no immunity, sought to strip the island of its gold. Years of fighting and unrest followed, as French colonists took over parts of the western side of the island and established huge sugar plantations, worked by African slaves. A revolution led to the formation of the republic of Haiti. By 1844, the Dominican Republic was formed, occupying two-thirds of the island. Fighting between the two neighbours raged, and the story of violence, unrest and hardship in Haiti and the Dominican Republic continues into modern times. Recently, the Dominican Republic has benefited from a huge growth in

tourism, and it has become more economically and politically stable, once again earning its right to be known as the paradise that enthralled Christopher Columbus.

In the modern Hispaniola, cuisine bears the hallmarks of Spanish and African influences and, as in neighbouring Cuba, a *sofrito* is the ubiquitous base of many dishes. Simple meals of fish, meat, rice and salad are enjoyed by families and tourists, who are now able to participate in the delights of a Hispaniolan kitchen.

Puerto Rico

Of all the Caribbean islands, Puerto Rico has a reputation of having maintained the strongest Spanish influence. It is the most easterly of the Greater Antilles and steeped in tradition; the city of Old San Juan, for example, was first built as a fortress and is still peppered with fifteenth-century buildings.

The Spaniards managed to maintain control of the island for hundreds of years, despite attempts by the British, French and Dutch to rout them. As a result of the Spanish-American War, Puerto Rico was ceded to the United States and now enjoys its status as a self-governing commonwealth.

Despite its long relationship with Spain, Puerto Rico – like other Caribbean islands – has become a melting pot of race, culture and religion. African slaves, Chinese and European immigrants, Cubans and others have all sought new lives on the island over 500 years, resulting in the mingling of culinary styles, and imported ingredients, which are almost a signature of Caribbean cooking. It is believed that indigenous Indians cooked with corn, seafood and tropical fruit, but the conquering Spanish introduced sugar cane, pork, beef, rice and olive oil. African slaves brought okra and taro.

Modern Puerto Ricans blend these ingredients with aplomb, creating an enormous variety of dishes that are often colourful and strongly aromatic. Meats are coated in a paste of *adobo*, which is made by crushing oregano, garlic, pepper, salt and peppercorns with olive oil and lime juice or vinegar. The *adobo* is thoroughly rubbed into the meat, which is then roasted, releasing an appetizing aroma as it cooks. Annatoo seeds are often added to Puerto Rican rice, stews and soups to give them a characteristic yellow colour. A particular festive favourite on the island is whole roasted pig, which is coated with sour orange juice before being barbecued and served with roasted green plantain and a sour garlic sauce.

Cayman Islands

The delightful Cayman Islands have much to offer tourists, but their culinary heritage is limited. These three islands (Grand Cayman, Little Cayman and Cayman Brac) have maintained strong links with Britain, Jamaica and the United States since they were first colonized, and they have not had the intimate relationship with the Spanish, Creole and French cultures which has benefited the cuisine of other Caribbean islands. Until the seventeenth century, the Caymans were largely uninhabited, and thereafter the most frequent visitors were shipwrecked sailors, pirates, deserters from the English Civil War and refugees.

Most modern-day Caymanians are of African, British or mixed Afro-British descent, and Jamaican influences dominate many dishes. Conch, a shellfish found in the sparkling shallow waters that surround the islands, is a staple and features in soups, stews and salads. Jerk seasonings are popular, and a traditional dessert of cake that has been soaked with locally made rum is a particular speciality. Tuna and marlin are found in deep waters nearby, but grouper and snapper are more common, and are used in soups or served with tomatoes, peppers and onions.

The development of a vernacular cooking style has been further impeded by the Islands' poor natural resources; agriculture is minimal and, although Caymanians enjoy one of the world's highest standards of living, 90 per cent of all foodstuffs has to be imported. Curiously, however, it was the availability of a particular type of food that first drew early travellers to the islands: marine turtles. In fact, Christopher Columbus first named the islands Las Tortugas after these large reptiles, which were common in the surrounding waters. (The islands were later renamed the Caymans after the caiman – a rare marine crocodile found in the region.) Subsequent over-exploitation of the Cayman Island green turtle population by fishermen nearly led to their demise, and they remain an endangered species worldwide.

At the tail end of the Bahamian archipelago a collection of more than 40 tropical islands and cays are sprinkled amidst a dazzling turquoise ocean. The crown colony of Turks and Caicos, like the Bahamas, was formed as part of a geological process that left these coral islands exposed above the sea when water levels dropped. The name 'caicos' is believed to derive from the Spanish word *cayos,* which means string of islands. These islands are composed of pale, flat rock and are encompassed by enormous stretches of fine ivory-white sand.

Turks

As agricultural opportunities are limited, the islanders rely heavily on the fruits of the sea, such as lobster and conch – the latter is often prepared with chopped onion and sweet peppers, lime juice and hot pepper sauce.

The first inhabitants of the islands were Amerindians, who lived peacefully, farming the land, until Europeans arrived in the late fifteenth century. Over the centuries, this small group of islands was ruled by the Bermudans, who established a salt industry here, the Spanish, the French, the Jamaicans and the British.

& Caicos Islands

Today, only 10 of the islands are inhabited, by fewer than 25,000 inhabitants. The population is swelled, however, by the ever-growing numbers of tourists who come to sample a Caribbean paradise. Local dishes include beef patties, which are made from pastry prepared with turmeric, and lean fried beef cooked with curry powder and green onions. Sauce for barbecued spare ribs, which feature prominently on menus around the Caribbean, is prepared in the Turks and Caicos using corn syrup, molasses, brown sugar and plenty of herbs and spices. The flavours in the mixture are allowed to infuse overnight before being poured thickly over pork ribs.

Caribbean

Cooking
Rice & Curry

The cuisine of the Caribbean has changed over time, but curried dishes have long been favourites, reflecting the islands' history of colonization and immigration.

When Indians brought their hot spices and fragrant curry powders to the region, they received an enthusiastic welcome, not least by the British contingent, who had developed a craving for curry in India. The original recipes called for lamb, which proved hard to find in the Caribbean, so goat meat was substituted. Like curries, rice dishes are ubiquitous in the region, and jambalaya (a Creole dish of rice with seafood, ham or chicken that is flavoured with herbs and spices) is a versatile and popular dish.

Rice & Papaya Salad

Papaya fruit (also know as 'pawpaw' or 'tree melon') is a true Caribbean favourite. Its delightfully sweet flavour is a joy in salads such as this, as well as in desserts.

Rinse and drain the rice, and pour into a saucepan. Add 450 ml/15 fl oz pint boiling salted water and the cinnamon stick. Bring to the boil, reduce the heat to a very low heat, cover and cook without stirring for 15–18 minutes, or until all the liquid is absorbed. The rice should be light and fluffy, and have steam holes on the surface. Remove the cinnamon stick and stir in the zest from 1 lime.

To make the dressing, put the remaining zest, lime and lemon juice, habañero chilli, hot pepper sauce and sugar in a food processor. Mix for a few minutes until blended. Alternatively, place all these ingredients in a screw-top jar and shake until well blended. Pour half the dressing over the hot rice and toss until the rice glistens.

Slice the papaya and mango into thin slices, then place in a bowl. Add the chopped green chilli, coriander and mint. Place the chicken on a chopping board, then remove and discard any skin or sinew. Cut into fine shreds and add to the bowl with the peanuts.

Add the remaining dressing to the chicken mixture and stir until all the ingredients are lightly coated. Spoon the rice onto a platter, pile the chicken mixture on top and serve with warm strips of pitta bread.

INGREDIENTS   Serves 4

- **175 g/6 oz easy-cook basmati rice**
- **1 cinnamon stick, bruised**
- **zest and juice of 2 limes**
- **zest and juice of 2 lemons**
- **1 habañero chilli, deseeded and finely chopped**
- **1–2 tbsp hot pepper sauce**
- **1 tbsp soft light brown sugar**
- **1 papaya, peeled and seeds removed**
- **1 mango, peeled and stone removed**
- **1 green chilli, deseeded and finely chopped**
- **2 tbsp freshly chopped coriander**
- **1 tbsp freshly chopped mint**
- **250 g/9 oz cooked chicken**
- **50 g/2 oz roasted peanuts, chopped**
- **strips of pitta bread, to serve**

HELPFUL HINT

The papaya or pawpaw's skin turns from green when unripe, through to yellow and orange. To prepare, cut in half lengthways, scoop out the black seeds with a teaspoon and discard. Cut away the thin skin before slicing.

New Orleans Jambalaya

The Caribbean has been heavily influenced by the diversity of peoples that have settled in the many islands, imparting their culture and cuisine. Here the Creole influence is represented in the well-known dish jambalaya.

Mix all the seasoning ingredients together in a small bowl and reserve.

Heat 2 tablespoons of the oil in a large flameproof casserole over a medium heat. Add the ham and sausage, and cook, stirring often, for 7–8 minutes until golden. Remove from the pan and reserve.

Add the remaining oil, onion, celery and peppers to the casserole and cook for about 4 minutes or until softened, stirring occasionally. Stir in the garlic, then, using a slotted spoon, transfer all the vegetables to a plate and reserve with the ham and sausage.

Add the chicken to the casserole and cook for about 4 minutes or until beginning to colour, turning once. Stir in the seasoning mix and turn the chicken pieces to coat well. Return the ham, sausage and vegetables to the casserole and stir well. Add the chopped tomatoes (with their juice, and the stock), and bring to the boil.

Stir in the rice and reduce the heat to low. Cover and simmer for 12 minutes. Uncover, stir in the spring onion and prawns, and cook, covered, for a further 4 minutes. Add the crab and gently stir in. Cook for 2–3 minutes, or until the rice is tender. Remove from the heat, cover and leave to stand for 5 minutes before serving (after having removed the bay leaves).

INGREDIENTS   Serves 6–8

For the Seasoning Mix

- **2 dried bay leaves**
- **1 tsp salt**
- **2 tsp cayenne pepper, or to taste**
- **2 tsp dried thyme**
- **1 tsp each ground white and black pepper, or to taste**

- **3 tbsp vegetable oil**
- **125 g/4 oz ham**
- **225 g/8 oz smoked pork sausage, cut into chunks**
- **2 large onions, peeled and chopped**
- **4 celery sticks, trimmed and chopped**
- **2 green peppers, deseeded and chopped**
- **2 garlic cloves, peeled and finely chopped**
- **350 g/12 oz skinless chicken breast fillets, diced**
- **400 g/ 14 oz can chopped tomatoes**
- **600 ml/1 pint fish stock**
- **400 g/14 oz long-grain white rice**
- **4 spring onions, trimmed and coarsely chopped**
- **275 g/10 oz raw prawns, peeled and deveined**
- **250 g/9 oz white crab meat**

Jambalayan-style Fried Rice

The Creole influence can be seen in this dish in the combination of sausage, chicken and shellfish. Modify the heat if preferred by reducing the amount of hot pepper sauce.

Put the rice, stock and bay leaves into a large saucepan and bring to the boil. Cover with a tight-fitting lid and simmer for 10 minutes over a very low heat. Remove from the heat and leave for a further 10 minutes.

Meanwhile, heat a large wok, then add the oil and heat. When hot, add the onion, green pepper, celery, garlic and oregano. Stir-fry for 6 minutes, or until all the vegetables have softened. Add the chicken and chorizo, and stir-fry for a further 6 minutes, or until lightly browned.

Add the tomato and cook over a medium heat for 2–3 minutes until collapsed. Stir in the prawns and hot pepper sauce and cook for a further 4 minutes, or until the prawns are cooked through. Stir in the cooked rice, spring onion and parsley, and season to taste with salt and pepper. Serve immediately.

INGREDIENTS   Serves 6

- **450 g/1 lb long-grain rice**
- **900 ml/1 $^1/_2$ pints hot chicken or fish stock**
- **2 fresh bay leaves**
- **2 tbsp vegetable oil**
- **2 medium onions, peeled and roughly chopped**
- **1 green pepper, deseeded and roughly chopped**
- **2 sticks celery, trimmed and roughly chopped**
- **3 garlic cloves, peeled and finely chopped**
- **1 tsp dried oregano**
- **300 g/11 oz skinless chicken breast fillets, chopped**
- **125 g/4 oz chorizo sausage, chopped**
- **3 tomatoes, peeled and chopped**
- **12 large raw prawns, peeled and deveined if preferred**
- **hot pepper sauce, to taste**
- **4 spring onions, trimmed and finely chopped**
- **2 tbsp freshly chopped parsley**
- **salt and freshly ground black pepper**

Calypso Rice with Curried Bananas

Traditionally Caribbean meals consist of fish, poultry or meat served with rice, beans or potatoes, plus one or two side dishes, which could include stir-fried vegetables and a rice dish such as this.

Heat the oil in a large frying pan and gently cook the onion for 10 minutes until soft. Add the garlic, chilli and red pepper, and cook for 2–3 minutes.

Rinse the rice under cold running water, then add to the pan and stir. Pour in the lime juice and stock, bring to the boil, cover and simmer for 12–15 minutes, or until the rice is tender and the stock is absorbed.

Stir in the black-eyed beans and parsley, and season to taste with salt and pepper. Leave to stand, covered, for 5 minutes before serving, to allow the beans to warm through.

While the rice is cooking, make the curried green bananas. Remove the skins from the bananas – they may need to be cut off with a sharp knife. Slice the flesh thickly. Heat the oil in a frying pan and cook the bananas, in 2 batches, for 2–3 minutes, or until lightly browned.

Pour the coconut milk into the pan and stir in the curry paste. Add the banana slices to the coconut milk and simmer, uncovered, over a low heat for 8–10 minutes, or until the bananas are very soft and the coconut milk slightly reduced.

Spoon the rice onto warmed serving plates, garnish with coriander and serve immediately with the curried bananas.

INGREDIENTS   Serves 4

- **2 tbsp vegetable oil**
- **1 medium onion, peeled and finely chopped**
- **1 garlic clove, peeled and crushed**
- **1 habañero chilli, deseeded and finely chopped**
- **1 red pepper, deseeded and finely chopped**
- **225 g/8 oz basmati rice**
- **juice of 1 lime**
- **350 ml/12 fl oz vegetable stock**
- **200 g/7 oz can black-eyed beans, drained and rinsed**
- **2 tbsp freshly chopped parsley**
- **salt and freshly ground black pepper**
- **sprigs of fresh coriander, to garnish**

For the Curried Bananas
- **4 green bananas**
- **2 tbsp vegetable oil**
- **2 tsp mild curry paste**
- **200 ml/7 fl oz coconut milk**

Spicy Mahi Mahi Rice

Caribbean waters are home to many varied and tropical fish, including mahi mahi, grouper, swordfish and snapper. If these are unavailable, use cod, whiting or monkfish.

Mix together the flour, coriander, allspice and chilli powder on a large plate. Coat the fish in the spice mixture, then place on a baking sheet, cover and chill in the refrigerator for 30 minutes.

Heat a large wok, then add 2 tablespoons of the oil and heat until almost smoking. Stir-fry the cashew nuts for 1 minute until browned, then remove and reserve.

Add a further 1 tablespoon of the oil and heat until almost smoking. Add the fish and stir-fry for 2 minutes. Using a fish slice, turn the fish pieces over and cook for a further 2 minutes until golden. Remove from the wok, place on a warm plate, cover and keep warm.

Add the remaining oil to the wok, heat until almost smoking, then stir-fry the spring onions and chilli for 1 minute before adding the carrot and peas, and stir-frying for a further 2 minutes. Stir in the rice, hot pepper sauce, soy sauce and reserved cashew nuts, and stir-fry for 3 more minutes. Add the fish, heat for 1 minute, then serve immediately.

INGREDIENTS   Serves 4

- 1 tbsp plain flour
- 1 tbsp freshly chopped coriander
- 1 tsp ground allspice
- 1 tsp chilli powder
- 550 g/1¼ lb thick-cut mahi mahi fillet (or cod), skinned and cut into large chunks
- 4 tbsp vegetable oil
- 50 g/2 oz cashew nuts
- 1 bunch of spring onions, trimmed and diagonally sliced
- 1 habañero chilli, deseeded and chopped
- 1 carrot, peeled and cut into matchsticks
- 125 g/4 oz frozen peas
- 450 g/1 lb cooked long-grain rice
- 2 tbsp hot pepper sauce
- 2 tbsp soy sauce

HELPFUL HINT

Care is needed when frying nuts, as they have a tendency to turn from golden to burnt very quickly. An alternative is to toast them on a baking sheet in the oven at 180°C/350°F/Gas Mark 4 for about 5 minutes until they are golden and fragrant.

Nutty Fruit Pilaf

The arrival of the many different cuisines to the Caribbean has resulted in a host of dishes that have been adapted to make the most of local produce. This can be seen in the liberal use of tropical fruits, for instance.

Melt half the butter in a saucepan or casserole dish with a tight-fitting lid. Add the cardamom pods and cinnamon stick, and cook for about 30 seconds before adding the bay leaves and rice. Stir well to coat the rice in the butter and add the stock. Bring to the boil, cover tightly and cook very gently for 15 minutes. Remove from the heat and leave to stand for a further 5 minutes.

Melt the remaining butter in a wok and, when foaming, add the onion, flaked almonds and pistachios. Stir-fry for 3–4 minutes until the nuts are beginning to brown. Remove and reserve.

Reduce the heat slightly and add the dried mango, papaya, figs and chicken, and continue stir-frying for a further 7–8 minutes until the chicken is cooked through. Return the nuts to the mixture and toss to mix.

Remove from the heat, then remove the cinnamon stick and bay leaves from the rice. Add the cooked rice to the chicken mixture and stir together well to mix. Season to taste with Tabasco sauce, salt and pepper. Garnish with parsley or coriander leaves, and serve immediately.

INGREDIENTS Serves 4–6

- **50 g/2 oz butter**
- **6 cracked green cardamom pods**
- **1 cinnamon stick, bruised**
- **2 bay leaves**
- **450 g/1 lb basmati rice**
- **600 ml/1 pint chicken stock**
- **1 onion, peeled and finely chopped**
- **50 g/2 oz flaked almonds**
- **50 g/2 oz shelled pistachios, roughly chopped**
- **125 g/4 oz ready-to-eat dried mangoes, roughly chopped**
- **50 g/2 oz ready-to-eat dried papaya, roughly chopped**
- **30 g/1 oz dried figs**
- **275 g/10 oz skinless chicken breast fillets, cut into chunks**
- **dash of Tabasco sauce**
- **salt and freshly ground black pepper**
- **fresh parsley or coriander leaves, to garnish**

Caribbean Goat Curry

Caribbean goat curry (or 'curry goat') is a popular dish, but does not always contain goat or kid. You are just as likely to find that lamb or mutton has been used.

Cut the meat into small cubes, discarding any fat or gristle. Place the meat in a bowl and sprinkle over the curry powder and ginger, together with the other spices. Add half the thyme and one of the bay leaves. Leave to marinate in the refrigerator for at least 4 hours, preferably overnight.

Heat the oil in a large heavy-based saucepan over a medium high heat. Remove the meat from the spice marinade, reserving any remaining marinade. Sauté the meat until sealed all over. Remove from the pan with a slotted spoon and reserve. Add the onion, garlic and chilli to the oil remaining in the pan and sauté for 5 minutes, stirring frequently. Return the meat to the pan together with the reserved marinade. Cook, stirring, for 3 minutes.

Blend the tomato purée with the stock and add to the pan together with a little salt and pepper and the remaining thyme and bay leaf. Bring to the boil, then reduce the heat to a simmer and cover with a lid.

Cook over a gentle heat for 1½ hours, or until the meat is very tender. Adjust seasoning if necessary, and stir in the chopped coriander. Remove the bay leaves. Serve garnished with the coriander sprigs accompanied by the freshly cooked rice.

INGREDIENTS   Serves 4

- **675 g/1 lb 8 oz boneless kid or goat meat**
- **1–2 tsp curry powder**
- **2.5 cm/1 inch piece of fresh root ginger, peeled and grated**
- **2 tsp ground turmeric**
- **1 tsp ground allspice**
- **a few sprigs of fresh thyme, leaves picked**
- **2 fresh bay leaves**
- **2 tbsp vegetable oil**
- **1 medium onion, peeled and chopped**
- **2 or 3 garlic cloves, peeled and chopped**
- **1 habañero chilli, deseeded and chopped**
- **1 tbsp tomato purée**
- **600 ml/1 pt lamb stock**
- **1 tbsp freshly chopped coriander sprigs, to garnish**
- **salt and freshly ground black pepper**
- **freshly cooked rice, to serve**

Coconut Fish Curry

This delicious curry is perfect when time is short and you need to prepare supper quickly. Why not enjoy a mojito cocktail while preparing the curry?

Put 1 tablespoon of the oil into a large frying pan and cook the onion, pepper and garlic for 5 minutes, or until soft. Add the remaining oil, curry paste, ginger and chilli, and cook for a further minute.

Pour in the coconut milk and bring to the boil. Reduce the heat and simmer gently for 5 minutes, stirring occasionally. Add the monkfish to the pan and continue to simmer gently for 5–10 minutes, or until the fish is tender, but not overcooked.

Meanwhile, cook the rice in a saucepan of boiling salted water for 15 minutes, or until tender. Drain the rice thoroughly and turn out into a serving dish.

Stir the chopped coriander and chutney gently into the fish curry, and season to taste with salt and pepper. Spoon the fish curry over the cooked rice, garnish with lime wedges and extra coriander sprigs, and serve immediately with spoonfuls of Greek yogurt and warm naan bread.

INGREDIENTS   Serves 4

- 2 tbsp vegetable oil
- 1 medium onion, peeled and very finely chopped
- 1 yellow pepper, deseeded and finely chopped
- 1 garlic clove, peeled and crushed
- 1 tbsp hot curry paste
- 2.5 cm/1 inch piece of root ginger, peeled and grated
- 1 habañero chilli, deseeded and finely chopped
- 400 ml/14 oz can coconut milk
- 700 g/1 1/2 lb firm white fish, e.g. monkfish fillets, skinned and cut into chunks
- 225 g/8 oz basmati rice
- 1 tbsp freshly chopped coriander plus extra spigs to garnish
- 1 tbsp mango chutney
- salt and freshly ground black pepper
- lime wedges, to serve
- Greek-style yogurt, to serve
- warm naan bread, to serve

Aromatic Chicken Curry

Whether roasted, fried, cooked in a curry or a stew, chicken is prepared with plenty of herbs and spices. A roast is very popular for a Sunday meal, while curries and stews are the normal mid-week fare.

Dry-roast the allspice and cinnamon in a large saucepan over a low heat for about 30 seconds. Stir in the curry paste.

Add the lentils to the saucepan with the bay leaf and lemon zest, then pour in the stock and add the Tabasco sauce. Stir, then slowly bring to the boil. Turn down the heat, half-cover the saucepan with a lid and simmer gently for 5 minutes, stirring occasionally.

Secure the chicken thighs with cocktail sticks to keep their shape. Place in the saucepan and half-cover. Simmer for 15 minutes.

Stir in the shredded spinach and cook for a further 25 minutes, or until the chicken is very tender and the sauce is thick. Remove the bay leaf and lemon zest. Stir in the coriander and lemon juice, then season to taste with salt and pepper. Serve immediately with the rice, lemon wedges and a little natural yogurt.

INGREDIENTS   Serves 4

- **2 tsp allspice**
- **1 tbsp ground cinnamon**
- **2 tsp hot curry paste**
- **125 g/4 oz red lentils, rinsed thoroughly and drained**
- **1 bay leaf**
- **small strip of lemon zest**
- **600 ml/1 pint chicken or vegetable stock**
- **Tabasco sauce, to taste**
- **8 chicken thighs, skinned**
- **175 g/6 oz spinach leaves, rinsed and shredded**
- **1 tbsp freshly chopped coriander**
- **2 tsp lemon juice**
- **salt and freshly ground black pepper**
- **freshly cooked rice, to serve**
- **lemon wedges, to serve**
- **low-fat plain yogurt, to serve**

HELPFUL HINT

Dry-roasting spices really releases the flavour and is a technique that can be used for many dishes. It is a particularly good way to flavour lean meat or fish. Try mixing dry-roasted spices with a little water or oil to make a paste. Spread the paste on meat or fish before baking to make a spicy crust.

Pumpkin & Chickpea Curry

This delicious dish has its origins in India – one of the many ethnic recipes that have been both adopted and adapted in the islands.

Heat the oil in a saucepan and add the onion. Fry gently for 5 minutes until softened. Add the garlic, ginger and spices, and fry for a further minute. Add the tomato and chilli, and cook for another minute.

Next add the pumpkin and curry paste, and fry gently for 3–4 minutes before adding the stock. Stir well, bring to the boil and simmer for 20 minutes until the pumpkin is tender.

Thickly slice the banana and add to the pumpkin along with the chickpeas. Simmer for a further 5 minutes. Season to taste with salt and pepper, and add the chopped coriander. Serve immediately, garnished with the extra coriander sprigs and accompanied by rice or flat bread.

INGREDIENTS   Serves 4

- 1 tbsp vegetable oil
- 1 small onion, peeled and sliced
- 2 garlic cloves, peeled and finely chopped
- 2.5 cm/1 inch piece of root ginger, peeled and grated
- 1 tsp ground allspice
- 1/2 tsp ground cloves
- 1/2 tsp ground turmeric
- 1 tsp ground cinnamon
- 2 tomatoes, chopped
- 2 habañero chillies, deseeded and finely chopped
- 450 g/1 lb pumpkin or butternut squash flesh, cubed
- 1 tbsp hot curry paste
- 300 ml/10 fl oz pint vegetable stock
- 1 large firm banana
- 400 g/14 oz can chickpeas, drained and rinsed
- salt and freshly ground black pepper
- 1 tbsp freshly chopped coriander plus extra sprigs, to garnish
- rice or flat bread, to serve

HELPFUL HINT

Curry pastes come in mild, medium and hot varieties. Although hot curry paste is recommended in this recipe, use whichever one you prefer.

Lobster & Prawn Curry

This delicious dish has a strong pungent flavour rather than an overpowering hot fiery taste – perfect to complement the shellfish used here. Serve with plenty of freshly cooked rice.

Using a sharp knife, slice the lobster meat thickly. Wash the tiger prawns and pat dry with absorbent kitchen paper. Make a small 1 cm/½ inch cut at the tail end of each prawn.

Heat a large wok, then add the oil and, when hot, stir-fry the lobster and tiger prawns for 4–6 minutes, or until pink. Using a slotted spoon, transfer to a plate and keep warm in a low oven.

Add the spring onion and stir-fry for 2 minutes, then stir in the garlic and ginger. Stir-fry for a further 2 minutes. Add the curry paste and stir-fry for another minute.

Pour in the coconut milk, lime zest and juice. Season to taste with salt and pepper. Bring to the boil and simmer for 1 minute. Return the prawns, lobster and any juices to the wok and simmer for 2 minutes. Stir in two-thirds of the freshly chopped coriander, garnished with the remaining coriander and accompanied by freshly cooked rice. Serve immediately.

INGREDIENTS   Serves 4

- **225 g/8 oz cooked lobster meat, shelled if necessary**
- **225 g/8 oz raw tiger prawns, peeled and deveined**
- **2 tbsp vegetable oil**
- **2 bunches of spring onions, trimmed and thickly sliced**
- **2 garlic cloves, peeled and chopped**
- **2.5 cm/1 inch piece of fresh root ginger, peeled and cut into matchsticks**
- **2 tbsp hot curry paste**
- **200 ml/7 fl oz coconut milk**
- **grated zest and juice of 1 lime**
- **3 tbsp freshly chopped coriander**
- **salt and freshly ground black pepper**
- **freshly cooked rice, to serve**
- **lemon wedges, to serve**

The Leeward
of the Le

Varied in geography and heritage, these islands, which are protected from the prevailing Atlantic winds, are united in their charm and beauty.

Islands
sser Antilles

The Virgin Islands

The cultural heritage of the Virgin Islands pays testament to the lives and times of the thousands of African slaves who were brought to the region to work on the sugar plantations. Many of them were taken from the African Gold Coast, and some modern-day islanders can trace their roots back 300 years. The islands have a palpable Afro-Caribbean flavour, and the food available reflects the basic diet of sweet potato, okra, cornmeal and breads that were the staples for slaves. Fresh fish is a firm favourite, and local varieties such as wahoo, yellowtail, grouper and red snapper – served with a hot lime sauce – are considered specialities. Virgin Island soups are, rather unusually, often flavoured with fruit and sweetened with sugar; the most famous of all soups in the region is the callaloo, which is made with a leafy vegetable similar to spinach.

Scattered in a crystal-blue sea, the Virgin Islands are green volcanic places renowned for their secluded beaches and isolated bays. These hideaways, in times past, provided an ideal place for pirates to lurk while waiting for passing cargo ships to plunder. There are around 90 islands altogether in the group, which are formed from the peaks of a row of submerged volcanoes which exploded from the ocean floor some 25 million years ago. British colonists developed large parts of the islands into sugar plantations, and about 50 of the islands and cays today form the British Virgin Islands (BVI), still retaining close links with Britain. Some of the remaining islands were known as the Danish West Indies until the First World War, when the United States bought the territory from Denmark to prevent the Germans from using the islands as a U-boat base. They now form the United States Virgin Islands.

Anguilla, Antigua

Fresh spiny lobsters, crayfish, yellowtail, whelks and red snapper are just some of the seafood enjoyed on the island of Anguilla, although here – as on many other Caribbean islands – fruit and vegetables to accompany the fish are often imported. This small island, a self-governing overseas territory of the United Kingdom, has a dry tropical climate, and its erratic rainfall makes agriculture difficult. Natural resources are few, but the inhabitants, who are mostly of African slave descent, have a reputation for being able to create some of the most elegant dishes in the region.

& Barbuda

In Antigua and Barbuda, the cuisine is noticeably spicier and more varied. The dishes display some Creole influences, despite these islands' long relationship with Britain, when large sugar-cane plantations were scattered across the interior of Antigua. Sauces may be pepper-hot, or spiced with curry powders from East India. Curried goat and spare ribs are perennial favourites on the islands, and may be served with breadfruit, yams or potatoes. A traditional dish is pepper pot: a spicy, tender stew of beef, pork and dumplings with okra. It is often served with fungi, an accompaniment made of cornmeal and okra, moulded into balls.

As elsewhere in the Caribbean, fried plantains appear on many menus; these vegetables are similar in appearance to bananas, but taste bitter and must be cooked before eating. They can be baked in the oven, or treated in much the same way as potatoes: mashed, fried or boiled. (On Spanish-speaking islands, they often appear as *tostones de plátano* and are fried, squashed and fried again until crispy.) Fresh fish feature in the local cuisine and, as grouper and snapper are still common in surrounding waters, they appear in many recipes. Blue marlin is hunted in deep waters, and is served pan-seared with lime juice or in a salad with curried pumpkin.

Dominica, Saint Martin & Environs

It has been said that the island of Dominica, the southernmost of the Leeward Islands in the Lesser Antilles, is the only place in the Caribbean that might still be recognized by Christopher Columbus if he were to return to the region today.

This is a dense, mountainous place with tropical forests and few sandy beaches to lure tourists and the large hotel operators. The island is lush and fertile, and, although varied fruit and vegetable crops are cultivated here, banana plantations have predominated. The Dominicans have paid a heavy price for this monoculture; when the price of bananas falls, or the crop is damaged by tropical storms, farmers struggle to survive.

French and British influences compete on the island today, but unusually there is a small region of native Carib people, the tribe that had settled on the island (and many others in the region) before Christopher Columbus arrived. As one might expect, the cuisine of Dominica reflects all these cultures, but it also has some rather unusual and distinctive dishes. 'Mountain chicken', for example, is a delicacy made from the flesh of a frog. Land crabs are also popular, and fresh seafood such as octopus, flying fish and spiny lobsters is readily available.

In Saint Martin, Dutch and other European influences have been brought to bear, but more traditional recipes include succulent meat curries, seafood seasoned with peppers, and stuffed crab. In Saint Barthélemy, the cuisine is mostly international, and few local dishes survive. Food is, nevertheless, is given a Caribbean lilt with mango sauces or Creole spices. Cuisine in Saba is unremarkable, being mostly continental and relying on imported ingredients. Regional cooking includes fresh seafood.

Montserrat, Saint Kitts & Saint Eustatius

Once known as an emerald island, rich and green, Montserrat sits in the southern range of the Leeward Islands and is, in nature, a verdant tropical island covered with fertile soil, rainforest and lush vegetation.

Its fortunes have changed spectacularly, however, in recent times. In 1995 the volcano of Soufrière burst into life after 350 years of dormancy and began to erupt, producing grey ash that fell over the southern part of the island. It continued its activity, which gradually grew in severity until 1997 – when a huge pyroclastic flow of high-speed lava destroyed seven villages and killed 19 people. Now the island's population is a fraction of what it once was (out of 11,000, only an estimated 4,000 remain). The people of Montserrat still serve their local cuisine to the tourists who come to view the active volcano, and the visitors are treated to the national dish of goat stew, known locally as goat water, served with large chunks of bread. Frog, also known as 'mountain chicken' is a traditional delicacy of the region.

Saint Kitts enjoys a good reputation for its local seafood, which is prepared by traditional Caribbean methods. Pepper pot stew, conch curry and spiny lobster are commonplace. The local drink is a liqueur, made from sugar cane and mixed with grapefruit soda. Traditional dishes of neighbouring Nevis included roasted and spiced suckling pig, and turtle (although this is now discouraged as turtles are endangered). Aubergine and avocados are used liberally and in many imaginative ways.

Known commonly as 'Statia', the little Dutch island of Saint Eustatius is steeped in a history that is being preserved for a burgeoning tourist trade. Its cuisine is varied, reflecting international tastes; Chinese food is particularly popular here, although some traditional Creole and Caribbean dishes are prepared, such as goat stew. Cheese plays an important part in local recipes, reflecting the influence of Dutch colonizers.

The Leeward French Antilles

Along with Martinique, the islands of Guadeloupe, La Désirade, Les Saintes and Marie-Galante make up the French Antilles, and are unmistakably Gallic in their culture and cuisine. There is, however, the usual potpourri of races in the French Antilles that is found elsewhere in the region; African, East Indian and British migrants have all added to the islands' heritage.

Of these islands, Guadeloupe possibly boasts the most exciting and imaginative of cuisines. Creole flavours dominate; the essence of Creole cooking is a fusion of French, Spanish and African ingredients and methods. The result is a powerful burst of flavour; meats are always well spiced, and sauces often have a tomato, garlic and herb base – there is little tradition of cooking with dairy products.

Seafood in Guadeloupe is treated with French delicacy of touch, and local herbs are added to enhance subtle flavours. A regional favourite is callaloo soup, made from leafy greens and herbs, and Colombo is a staple here. This tender meat or poultry stew is made with sweet potato, pumpkin, herbs, spices and rice. It is named after the capital of Sri Lanka – workers migrated from here to tend the sugar plantations, and brought their strong spices with them.

The little islands of La Désirade, Les Saintes and Marie-Galante lie in the warm tropical waters around the larger, busier Guadeloupe. They offer tranquillity, with beautiful beaches and spectacular coral reefs; however, there is little local produce as the landscape is mostly arid with poor soil. Local dishes include court-bouillon – a dish made from poached fish served with

lime, wine, potatoes and onion – and accra – balls of locally caught fish and chillies, deep-fried in batter.

Caribbean

Cooking Fish & Seafood

It is no wonder that the islands of the Caribbean, buffeted as they are by the waves of the Atlantic Ocean and Caribbean Sea, are home to a range of dishes inspired by fish and other seafood.

Most of the fish in the region are small reef fish, however, which cannot be caught in large enough numbers for commercial enterprises, so some of the fish used by the islanders has to be imported. Even the ubiquitous red snapper, found in the coastal waters and near reefs in this region, have been overfished to such an extent that other similar species are now sometimes substituted in traditional recipes.

Gingered Cod Steaks

Nowadays tourism is the main industry of most of the Caribbean islands, and this is reflected in the cosmopolitan menus found in most tourist hotels. This recipe is a reflection of this international aspect of the islands' cuisine.

Preheat the grill to a medium heat and line the grill rack with a layer of foil. Coarsely grate the piece of ginger. Mix the spring onion, ginger, parsley and sugar. Add 1 tablespoon water.

Pat the fish steaks dry with kitchen towel. Season to taste with salt and pepper. Place on 4 separate 20.5 x 20.5 cm/ 8 x 8 inch foil squares. Carefully spoon the spring onion mixture over the fish. Dot the butter place over the fish. Loosely fold the foil over the steaks to enclose the fish and to make a parcel.

Place the parcels under the preheated grill and cook for 10–12 minutes, or until the fish is cooked and the flesh has turned opaque. Place the fish parcels on individual serving plates. Serve immediately with the fresh vegetables.

INGREDIENTS   Serves 4

- **4 spring onions, trimmed and cut into thin strips**
- **2.5 cm /1 inch piece of fresh root ginger, peeled and coarsely grated**
- **2 tsp freshly chopped parsley**
- **1 tbsp soft brown sugar**
- **4 x 175 g /6 oz thick cod steaks**
- **25 g/1 oz butter cut into small cubes**
- **salt and freshly ground black pepper**
- **hot pepper sauce, to serve**
- **freshly cooked vegetables, to serve**

HELPFUL HINT

Why not serve this dish with roasted new potatoes en papillote. Place the new potatoes into double-thickness greaseproof paper with a few cloves of peeled garlic. Drizzle with a little olive oil and season well with salt and black pepper. Fold all the edges of the greaseproof paper together and roast in the oven at 180°C/350°F/Gas Mark 4 for 40–50 minutes before serving in the paper casing.

Barbecued Fish Kebabs

What could be a better way to relax and enjoy yourself than inviting friends round and cooking these kebabs on the barbecue? Only being on the beach in the Caribbean eating them ...

If using wooden skewers, soak in cold water for 30 minutes to prevent them from catching alight during cooking.

Meanwhile, prepare the sauce. Put the fish stock, tomato ketchup, Worcestershire sauce, vinegar, sugar, Tabasco and tomato purée in a small saucepan. Stir well and leave to simmer for 5 minutes.

When ready to cook the kebabs, line a grill rack with a single layer of foil and heat the grill to high. Drain the skewers, if necessary, then thread the fish chunks, quartered red onions and cherry tomatoes alternately on to the skewers. Season the kebabs to taste with salt and pepper, and brush with the sauce.

Grill under the hot grill for 8–10 minutes, basting with the sauce occasionally during cooking. Turn the kebabs often to ensure that they are cooked thoroughly and evenly on all sides. Serve immediately with couscous.

INGREDIENTS   Serves 4

For the Sauce
- **150 ml /5 fl oz pint fish stock**
- **5 tbsp tomato ketchup**
- **2 tbsp Worcestershire sauce**
- **2 tbsp wine vinegar**
- **2 tbsp soft brown sugar**
- **2 drops of hot pepper sauce**
- **2 tbsp tomato purée**

- **450 g/1 lb herring or mackerel fillets, cut into chunks**
- **2 small red onions, peeled and quartered**
- **16 cherry tomatoes**
- **salt and freshly ground black pepper**

HELPFUL HINT

If using a barbecue, light it at least 20 minutes before use in order to allow the coals to heat up properly. (The coals will be coated with a grey-white ash when ready.) Barbecue some peppers and red onions, and serve with a mixed salad as an accompaniment to the fish kebabs.

Hot Salsa-filled Sole

Salsas originated in Latin America and originally consisted of 4 or 5 ingredients, mainly tomatoes and chillies. As salsas became more popular, cooks became more experimental, as this recipe shows.

First make the salsa. Put all the salsa ingredients in a small bowl. Season to taste with salt and pepper. Mix thoroughly and let stand for 30 minutes to allow the flavours to develop.

Lay the fish fillets on a board skin-side up and pile the salsa on the tail end of the fillets. Fold the fillets in half, season and place in a large shallow frying pan. Pour over the orange and lemon juice.

Bring to a gentle boil, then reduce the heat to a simmer. Cover and cook over a low heat for 7–10 minutes, adding a little water if the liquid is evaporating. Remove the cover, add the mint and cook uncovered for a further 3 minutes. Garnish with the lime wedges and serve immediately with the salad leaves.

INGREDIENTS   Serves 4

For the Salsa
- 1 small mango peeled, stoned and finely chopped
- 8 cherry tomatoes, quartered
- 1 small red onion, peeled and finely chopped
- pinch of sugar
- 1 red chilli, deseeded, stoned and finely chopped
- 2 tbsp white wine vinegar
- zest and juice of 1 lime
- 1 tbsp olive oil
- sea salt and freshly ground black pepper

- 8 x 175 g/6 oz lemon sole fillets, skinned
- 150 ml/5 fl oz pint orange juice
- 2 tbsp lemon juice
- 2 tbsp freshly chopped mint
- lime wedges, to garnish
- salad leaves, to serve

HELPFUL HINT
To temper the hotness of the salsa, add 1–2 teaspoons warmed clear honey.

Tuna Chowder

The Caribbean abounds in fresh fish and there are many delicious version of this classic chowder. Use a variety of seafood or, if preferred, stick to your favourite fish and enjoy a satisfying and healthy meal.

Heat the oil in a large heavy-based saucepan. Add the onion and celery, and gently cook for about 5 minutes, stirring from time to time until the onion is softened. Next stir in the tuna and cook for 2 minutes. Stir in the flour and cook for about 1 minute to thicken.

Draw the pan off the heat and gradually pour in the milk, stirring throughout. Add the drained sweetcorn and the thyme. Mix gently, then bring to the boil. Cover and simmer for 5 minutes.

Remove the pan from the heat and season to taste with salt and pepper. Sprinkle the chowder with the cayenne pepper and chopped parsley. Divide into soup bowls and serve immediately.

INGREDIENTS   Serves 4

- **2 tsp vegetable oil**
- **1 onion, peeled and finely chopped**
- **2 celery sticks, trimmed and finely sliced**
- **300 g/10 oz fresh tuna steak, cut into small pieces**
- **1 tbsp plain flour**
- **600 ml/1 pint semi-skimmed milk**
- **320 g/11 oz can sweetcorn in water, drained**
- **2 tsp freshly chopped thyme**
- **pinch of cayenne pepper**
- **2 tbsp freshly chopped parsley**
- **salt and freshly ground black pepper**

Sweetcorn & Crab Soup

A delicious example of Caribbean culinary fusion, where the tastes of the Orient and the Caribbean have blended to provide a tasty soup.

Rinse the corn cobs and pat dry with absorbent kitchen paper. Using a sharp knife and holding the corn cobs at an angle to the cutting board, cut down along the cobs to remove the kernels, then scrape the cobs to remove any excess milky residue. Put the kernels and the milky residue into a large wok.

Add the chicken stock to the wok and place over a high heat. Bring to the boil, stirring and pressing some of the kernels against the side of the wok to squeeze out the starch to help thicken the soup. Simmer for 15 minutes, stirring occasionally.

Add the spring onion, ginger, rum, soy sauce and brown sugar to the wok, and season to taste with salt and pepper. Simmer for a further 5 minutes, stirring occasionally.

Blend the cornflour with 1 tablespoon cold water to form a smooth paste and whisk into the soup. Return to the boil, then simmer over a medium heat until thickened.

Add the crabmeat, stirring until blended. Beat the egg white with the chilli-flavoured oil and stir into the soup in a slow steady stream, stirring constantly. Stir in the chopped coriander and serve immediately.

INGREDIENTS — Serves 4

- **450 g/1 lb fresh corn on the cob**
- **1.3 litres/2 ¼ pints chicken stock**
- **2 or 3 spring onions, trimmed and finely chopped**
- **1 cm/½ inch piece of fresh root ginger, peeled and finely chopped**
- **1 tbsp rum**
- **2–3 tsp soy sauce**
- **1 tsp soft light brown sugar**
- **2 tsp cornflour**
- **225 g/8 oz white crabmeat, fresh or canned**
- **1 medium egg white**
- **1 tsp chilli-flavoured oil**
- **1–2 tbsp freshly chopped coriander**
- **salt and freshly ground black pepper**

HELPFUL HINT

If liked, add 1–2 tablespoons of hot pepper sauce to the soup before stirring in the egg white and oil.

Coconut Seafood

Carnival is the highlight of the year on the Caribbean islands – great feasting is enjoyed when sumptuous dishes are served. This seafood dish is an ideal choice to help the celebrations go with a swing.

Heat a large wok, add the oil and heat until it is almost smoking, swirling the oil around the wok to coat the sides. Add the prawns and stir-fry over a high heat for 4–5 minutes, or until browned on all sides. Using a slotted spoon, transfer the prawns to a plate and keep warm in a low oven.

Add the spring onion, garlic, chilli and ginger to the wok and stir-fry for 1 minute. Add the mushrooms and stir-fry for a further 3 minutes. Using a slotted spoon, transfer the mushroom mixture to a plate and keep warm in a low oven.

Add the wine and coconut milk to the wok, bring to the boil and boil rapidly for 4 minutes, until reduced slightly.

Return the mushroom mixture and prawns to the wok, bring back to the boil, then simmer for 1 minute, stirring occasionally, until piping hot. Stir in the freshly chopped coriander and season to taste with salt and pepper. Serve immediately with the freshly cooked rice.

INGREDIENTS   Serves 4

- **2 tbsp vegetable oil**
- **450 g/1 lb raw king prawns, peeled and deveined**
- **2 bunches of spring onions, trimmed and thickly sliced**
- **1 garlic clove, peeled and chopped**
- **1 green chilli, deseeded and finely chopped**
- **2.5 cm/1 inch piece of fresh root ginger, peeled and cut into matchsticks**
- **125 g/4 oz fresh shiitake mushrooms, rinsed and halved**
- **150 ml/5 fl oz dry white wine**
- **200 ml/7 fl oz carton coconut milk**
- **4 tbsp freshly chopped coriander**
- **salt and freshly ground black pepper**
- **freshly cooked rice, to serve**

Creamy Coconut Seafood Pasta

When buying a coconut it is important to ensure that it is fresh as possible. The coconut needs to feel heavy in relation to its size, and there should be the sound of splashing when it is shaken. Pick up a few coconuts to compare – the lighter the coconut, the less liquid inside and therefore the older the nut.

Bring a large pan of lightly salted water to a rolling boil. Add the pasta and cook according to the packet instructions, or until al dente.

Meanwhile, heat the vegetable and chilli-flavoured oils together in a saucepan. Add the spring onion, garlic, chilli and ginger, and cook for 3–4 minutes, or until softened.

Blend the coconut milk and cream together in a jug. Add the prawns and crabmeat to the pan and stir over a low heat for a few seconds to heat through. Gradually pour in the coconut cream mixture, stirring all the time.

Stir the chopped coriander into the seafood sauce and season to taste with salt and pepper. Continue heating the sauce gently until piping hot, but do not allow to boil.

Drain the pasta thoroughly and return to the pan. Add the seafood sauce and gently toss together to coat the pasta. Tip into a warmed serving dish or spoon onto individual plates. Serve immediately, garnished with coriander sprigs.

INGREDIENTS   Serves 4

- **400 g/14 oz egg tagliatelle**
- **1 tsp vegetable oil**
- **1 tsp chilli-flavoured oil**
- **4 spring onions, trimmed and sliced diagonally**
- **1 garlic clove, peeled and crushed**
- **1 habañero chilli, deseeded and finely chopped**
- **2.5 cm/1 inch piece of fresh root ginger, peeled and grated**
- **150 ml/5 fl oz coconut milk**
- **100 ml/3$^1/_2$ fl oz double cream**
- **225 g/8 oz cooked peeled tiger prawns**
- **185 g/6$^1/_2$ oz fresh white crabmeat**
- **2 tbsp freshly chopped coriander plus extra sprigs to garnish**
- **salt and freshly ground black pepper**

HELPFUL HINT

Coconut milk can be bought either in cans or long-life cartons, or you can make it yourself if you prefer. Put 125 g/4 oz desiccated coconut into a food processor or blender with 225 ml/8 fl oz boiling water and process for 30 seconds. Leave to cool for 5 minutes, then tip into a sieve lined with muslin over a bowl. Allow to drain for a few minutes, then squeeze out as much liquid as possible. Discard the coconut. If preferred, use all coconut milk rather than the coconut milk and double cream.

Grilled Snapper with Roasted Pepper

Not only does this look and taste good, but also it's ready in next to no time. Serve it with a salad and pasta for a delicious quick and easy supper.

Preheat the grill to a high heat and line the bottom of the grill rack with foil. Cut the tops off the peppers and divide into quarters. Remove the seeds and membrane, then place on the foil-lined grill rack and cook for 8–10 minutes, turning frequently, until the skins have become charred and blackened. Remove from the grill rack, place in a polythene bag and leave until cool. When the peppers are cool, strip off and discard the skin. Slice the flesh thinly and reserve.

Cover the grill rack with another piece of foil, then place the snapper fillets skin-side up on the grill rack. Season to taste with salt and pepper, and brush with a little of the olive oil. Cook for 10–12 minutes, turning over once and brushing again with a little olive oil.

Pour the cream and wine into a small saucepan, bring to the boil and simmer for about 5 minutes until the sauce has thickened slightly. Add the chopped dill, season to taste and stir in the reserved peppers. Arrange the cooked snapper fillets on warm serving plates and pour over the cream and pepper sauce. Garnish with the extra dill sprigs and serve immediately with the freshly cooked tagliatelle.

INGREDIENTS   Serves 4

- 1 medium red pepper
- 1 medium green pepper
- 4–8 snapper fillets, depending on size, about 450 g/1 lb
- 1 tbsp olive oil
- 5 tbsp double cream
- 125 ml/4 fl oz white wine
- 1 tbsp freshly chopped dill plus extra sprigs, to garnish
- sea salt and freshly ground black pepper
- freshly cooked tagliatelle, to serve

Ackee and Saltfish

Ackee fruit is pear-shaped and, when ripening, turns from green to bright red, then to yellow-orange. It splits open to reveal three black shiny seeds surrounded by a soft creamy, spongy white-yellow flesh. This is Jamaica's national dish and often served with boiled green bananas as well as fried dumplings.

Place the salted cod in a large bowl and cover with cold water. Leave for at least 24 hours, changing the water at least 6 times. Rinse thoroughly. When ready to cook, place in a saucepan and cover with cold water. Bring to the boil, then simmer for 15 minutes, or until tender.

If using canned ackee, drain when required. If using fresh, discard the seeds and pink membrane, wash the ackee thoroughly and place in medium saucepan. Cover with water and bring to the boil. Reduce the heat to a simmer and cook for 15–20 minutes, or until tender. Drain and reserve.

Remove the fish from the pan and immerse in cold water, then drain and leave until cool enough to handle. Once cool, remove and discard any bones and skin from the fish. Flake the flesh into small pieces and reserve.

Heat the butter and oil in a large frying pan over a medium heat. Add the onion and garlic. Once softened a little, add the thyme, tomato, chilli and allspice. Cook for 3–4 minutes, stirring frequently.

Add the flaked fish and cook for a further 5 minutes before adding the ackee. Cook for another 5–8 minutes, stirring carefully so as not to crush the ackee. Season to taste with the black pepper and sprinkle with the spring onion. Serve if liked with fried dumplings or boiled green bananas.

INGREDIENTS   Serves 4

- **450 g/1 lb salted cod**
- **540 g/1lb 6 oz can ackee or 4 ripe ackee**
- **25 g/1 oz butter**
- **25 ml/1 fl oz vegetable oil**
- **1 medium onion, peeled and chopped**
- **2–3 garlic cloves, peeled and chopped**
- **2 sprigs of fresh thyme**
- **225 g/8 oz ripe tomatoes**
- **1 habañero chilli, deseeded and sliced**
- **1 tsp ground allspice**
- **freshly ground black pepper**
- **2 spring onions, trimmed and chopped**

HELPFUL HINT

Ackee tastes similar to scrambled eggs. It is banned from being imported into many countries because of its possible toxicity.

Louisiana Prawns & Fettuccine

The term Creole is applied to dishes that come from both the Caribbean and the Southern states of the United States, particularly Louisiana. Creole cooking has hints of French, Spanish and often African cuisines. This is just such a recipe.

Heat 2 tablespoons of the oil in a large saucepan over a high heat and add the reserved prawn shells and heads. Fry for 2–3 minutes, until the shells turn pink and are lightly browned. Add half the shallot, half the garlic, the chilli, half the basil and the carrot, onion, celery, parsley and thyme. Season lightly with salt, pepper and cayenne, and sauté for 2–3 minutes, stirring often.

Pour in the wine and stir, scraping the pan well. Bring to the boil and simmer for 1 minute, then add the tomato. Cook for a further 3–4 minutes. Pour in 200 ml/7 fl oz water. Bring to the boil, reduce the heat and simmer for about 30 minutes, stirring often and using a wooden spoon to mash the prawn shells and release as much flavour as possible. Lower the heat if the sauce is reducing too quickly.

Strain through a sieve, pressing well to extract as much liquid as possible; there should be about 450 ml/15 fl oz. Pour the liquid into a clean pan and bring to the boil. Reduce the heat and simmer gently until the liquid is reduced by about half.

Heat the remaining oil over a high heat in a clean frying pan and add the peeled prawns. Season lightly and add the lemon juice. Cook for 1 minute, lower the heat and add the remaining shallot and garlic. Cook for 1 minute. Add the sauce and adjust the seasoning.

Meanwhile, bring a large pan of lightly salted water to a rolling boil and add the fettuccine. Cook, or until al dente. Drain thoroughly. Transfer to a warmed serving dish, add the sauce and toss well. Garnish with the remaining basil and serve immediately.

INGREDIENTS   Serves 4

- **4 tbsp vegetable oil**
- **450 g/1 lb raw tiger prawns, rinsed and peeled, shells and heads reserved**
- **2 shallots, peeled and finely chopped**
- **4 garlic cloves, peeled and finely chopped**
- **1 habañero chilli, deseeded and finely chopped**
- **large handful of fresh basil leaves**
- **1 carrot, peeled and finely chopped**
- **1 onion, peeled and finely chopped**
- **1 celery stick, trimmed and finely chopped**
- **2 or 3 sprigs of fresh parsley**
- **2 or 3 sprigs of fresh thyme**
- **salt and freshly ground black pepper**
- **pinch of cayenne pepper**
- **175 ml/6 fl oz dry white wine**
- **450 g/1 lb ripe tomatoes, roughly chopped**
- **juice of $^1/_2$ lemon, or to taste**
- **350 g/12 oz fettuccine**

The Windward
of the Le

Steep volcanic peaks and wide expanses of sandy beach identify the
Windward Islands as fertile, lush places with tasty offerings for the cooking pot.

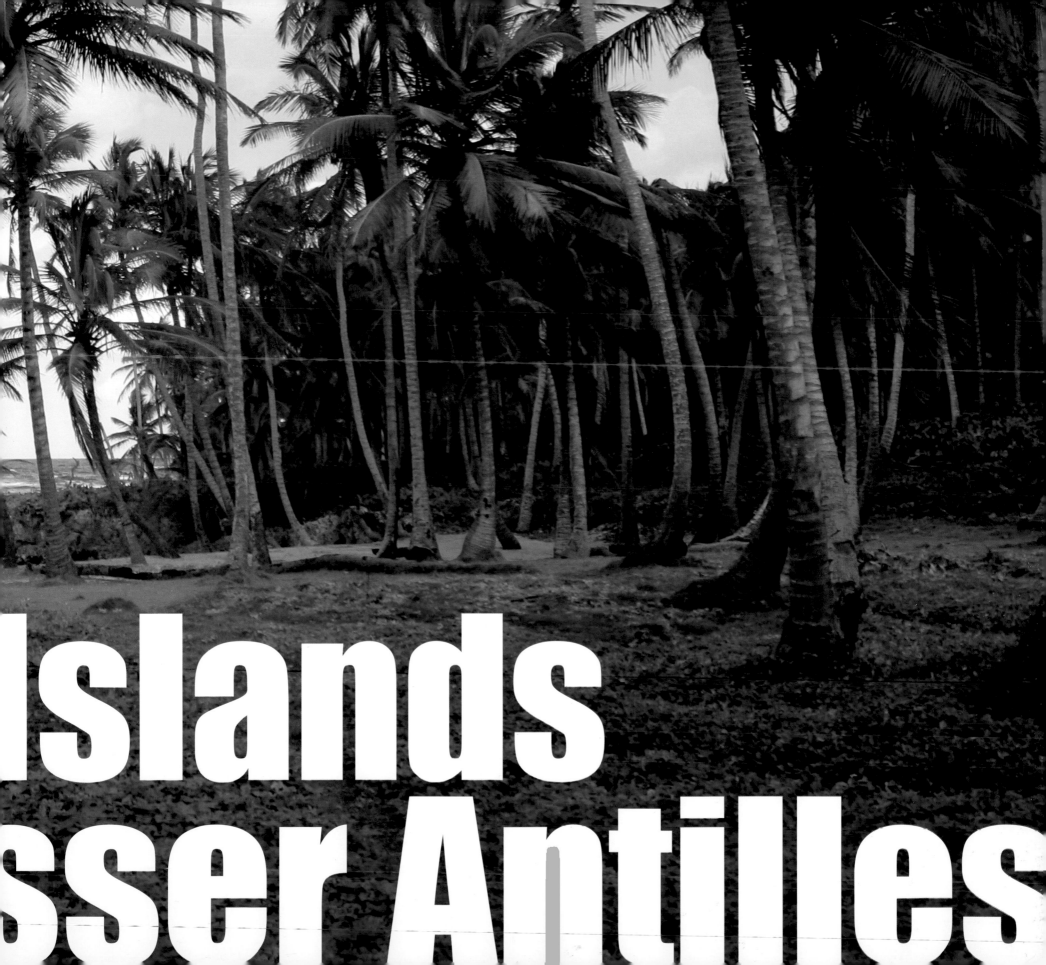

Islands
sser Antilles

Barbados

The Caribbean paradise of Barbados may be known as 'Little England' locally, but its cuisine reflects a far wider range of influences and Bajans owe little to the British in terms of food. The island's first inhabitants were migrants from South America, including the Arawak and Carib Indians, although the island is believed to have been uninhabited by the fifteenth century when the Spanish arrived. The British landed in the 1620s and, uniquely, maintained their rule of this Caribbean island until independence in 1966. Thousands of Africans were brought to Barbados as slaves, and many Celts from Ireland and Scotland migrated to the Island to work as servants, all adding to the ethnic mix that now exists on the island.

The island enjoys a tropical climate and, although many areas have been developed and urbanized, areas of wild rainforest, marsh and mangrove swamp survive intact. Sugar cane still dominates much of the agriculture, but a large variety of vegetables and fruits, such as papaya, passion fruit and mango, are grown on the island, sold at the lively markets. They feature in the culinary delights on offer to both locals and the many tourists who visit this popular island. Rum and molasses are by-products of the sugar cane, and these have come to feature in Bajan dishes. Traditional fare includes the ubiquitous flying fish, which is served in a variety of ways, including boiled, stewed and fried. Cooked well, it is moist and has a delicate nutty flavour, and it is often served with a yellow sauce of mustard and onions. A store cupboard essential is the Bajan seasoning mix, made from a blend of chopped onions, Scotch bonnet peppers and garlic mixed with herbs, seasoning, vinegar and Worcestershire sauce. This seasoning is left for a week to mature, before being rubbed on meat, poultry or fish.

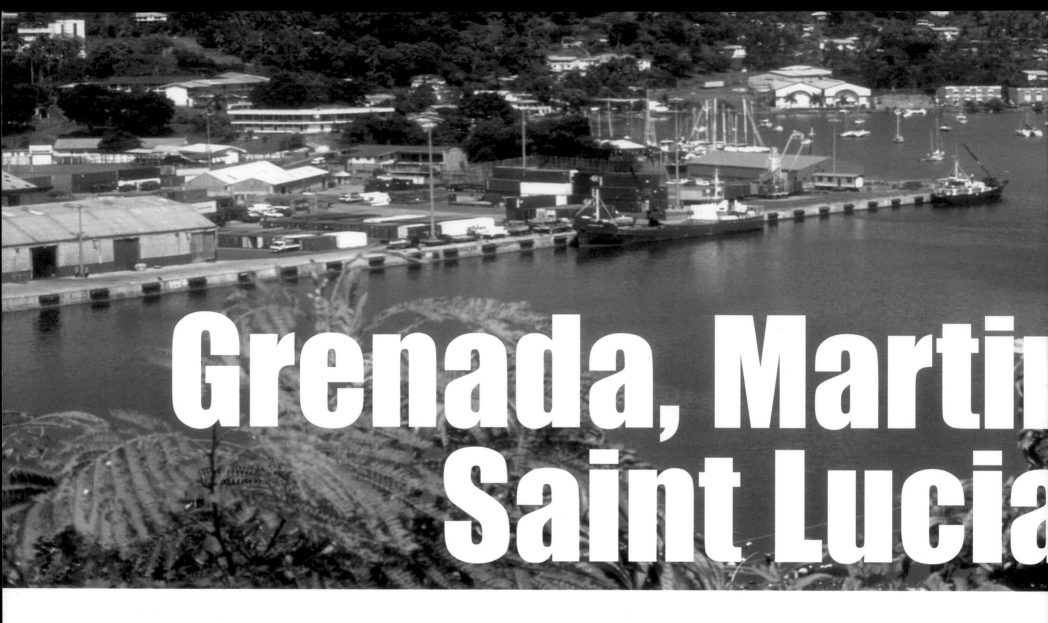

Grenada, Martinique, Saint Lucia

Grenada has been fittingly called the Caribbean spice island, for here an array of spices is cultivated for local use and export. While other Caribbean islands also grow spices, Grenada's climate and landscape particularly suit their production on a larger scale.

The bushy nutmeg tree produces two spices; mace and nutmeg. (Finely powdered nutmeg is often added to rum punch.) Cocoa trees also proliferate in the fertile soil and, during the months of January and February,

the hillsides light up with flaming orange flowers which bloom in unison. Clove and cinnamon are locally produced, as is allspice, the dried unripe berry of the pimento tree which itself has hints of cinnamon, cloves and nutmeg. It is sprinkled liberally on meat, added to stews or used to create jerk seasoning.

With the exception of Martinique, the Windward Islands were colonial outposts of Britain, and remain within the British Commonwealth. Martinique, however, has remained in French hands, almost without break, since 1635. The food of the island is widely regarded as some of the best in the Caribbean, combining, as it does, African, Creole and French culinary arts.

que,
& Saint Vincent

This marriage of cuisines owes much to the blending of intoxicating spices, fresh seafood and meat, and home-grown tangy fruits. Favourite dishes include chadron, which is sea urchin, and blaff, a dish of freshly poached fish and hot peppers in clear stock.

Saint Lucia's historical battle between the British and French is, thankfully, not played out with its food, which retains its own distinctive quality. Pumpkin soup is served in small eateries, while lobster, flying fish and breadfruit are cooked over hot coals. Pouile dudon – a dish of chicken cooked in coconut and sugar – is a speciality. The food of St Vincent and the Grenadines has a less

pronounced character, although it is hearty and simple – made from the fresh fruit and vegetables that grow well in these fertile islands.

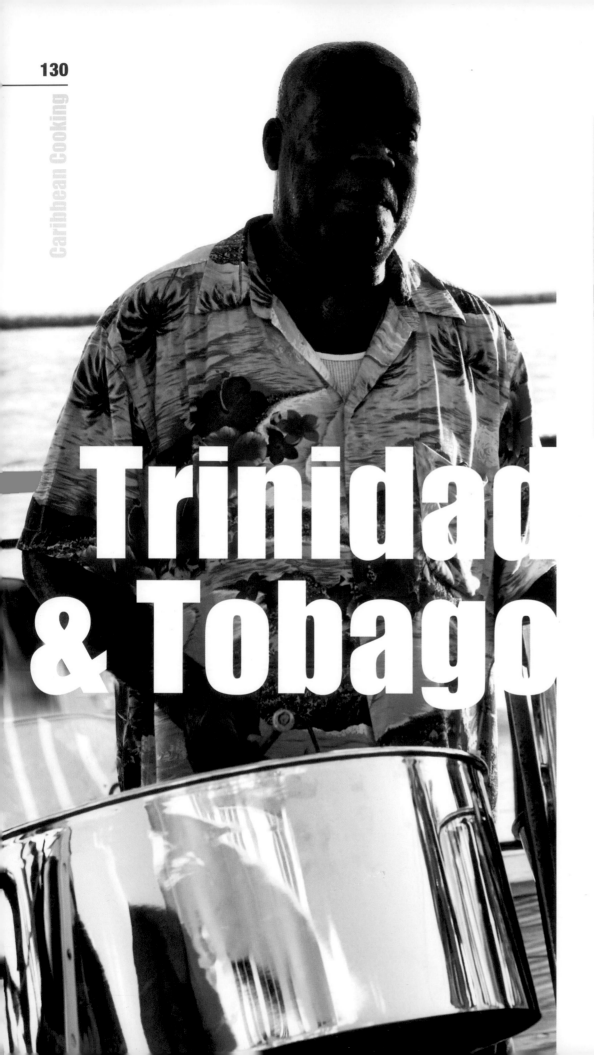

Trinidad & Tobago

Trinidad and its tiny neighbour, Tobago, form a single nation and are the most southerly of all Caribbean islands. In fact, Trinidad lies close to the coast of Venezuela, to which it was connected just 10,000 years ago.

Christopher Columbus was probably the first European to set foot on the beautiful island of Trinidad, in 1498. The Spanish took control of the island in 1592, and the British captured Trinidad and Tobago from them in 1797, although fierce battles for colonial rights continued between European powers for many years. The British finally relinquished power in 1962, when Trinidad and Tobago gained nationhood. The islands were dubbed the 'Rainbow Country' by Desmond Tutu, in celebration of the nation's diversity. Islanders can trace their roots to places as faraway as Europe, Africa, China, India and the Middle East, a fact that is evident in the full range of Indian, Jamaican, Creole, Chinese and European dishes that are prepared on the islands.

This hotchpotch of people, races, creeds and languages unite at carnival time, when the sound of steel bands resonates through the streets of Trinidad, and its capital, Port-of-Spain, becomes a swirling whirling spectacle of colours, costumes and calypso. It was in Trinidad that calypso developed from the traditional folk songs of African/West Indian immigrants, and these lyrical songs use satire, banter and innuendo to tell the story of the people's hopes and hardships.

While Trinidad is famous for its energy, diversity, vibrancy and bustling business centre, its neighbour Tobago is a more traditional Caribbean island. The lifestyle here is predominantly rural, and a calming wind prevails across the island, encouraging a more leisurely approach to daily chores. Tobago's tranquillity is reflected in a beautiful landscape that has been largely undisturbed by tourism, with interior rainforest and deserted coastal coves and sandy beaches.

Caribbean

Cooking
Meat & Poultry

Many of the meat and poultry dishes of the Caribbean have been passed down from generation to generation, and hark back to the days before refrigeration.

To prevent meat from going bad in the hot tropical sun, a number of techniques were used. Salting, for example, can preserve meat for some time, and salted pork is a traditional Caribbean dish. Stewing meat (especially goat) and poultry to a point of melting succulence, marinating it in acidic liquids (such as vinegar, lime juice or lemon juice) or rubbing it with hot spices are all popular ways of adding intense flavours or tenderizing tough meat.

Jamaican Jerk Pork with Rice & Peas

Rice and peas is one of the all-time classics of the Caribbean. Originally fresh pigeon peas were used, but, as these are seasonal, more often dried red kidney beans are substituted.

Soak the red kidney beans in plenty of cold water overnight.

To make the jerk pork marinade, purée the onion, garlic, lime juice, molasses, soy sauce, ginger, chilli, cinnamon, allspice and nutmeg together in a food processor until smooth. Put the pork chops into a plastic or non-reactive dish and pour over the marinade, turning the chops to coat. Marinate in the refrigerator for at least 1 hour or overnight.

Drain the beans and place in a large saucepan with about 2 litres/3½ pints cold water. Bring to the boil and continue boiling rapidly for 10 minutes. Reduce the heat, cover and simmer gently, for 1 hour until tender, adding more water if necessary. When cooked, drain well and mash roughly.

Heat the oil for the rice over a medium heat in a saucepan with a tight-fitting lid and add the onion, celery and garlic. Cook gently for 5 minutes until softened. Add the bay leaves, rice and stock, and stir. Bring to the boil, cover and cook very gently for 10 minutes. Add the beans and stir well again. Cook for a further 5 minutes, then remove from the heat.

Heat a griddle pan until almost smoking. Remove the pork chops from the marinade, scraping off any surplus, and add to the hot pan. Cook for 5–8 minutes on each side, or until cooked. Garnish with the parsley and serve immediately with the rice.

INGREDIENTS   Serves 4

- **175 g/6 oz dried red kidney beans**
- **2 onions, peeled and chopped**
- **2 garlic cloves, peeled and crushed**
- **4 tbsp lime juice**
- **2 tbsp each dark molasses, soy sauce and chopped fresh root ginger**
- **2 jalapeño chillies, deseeded and chopped**
- **½ tsp ground cinnamon**
- **¼ tsp each ground allspice and ground nutmeg**
- **4 pork loin chops, on the bone**
- **sprigs of fresh flat-leaf parsley, to garnish**

For the Rice
- **1 tbsp vegetable oil**
- **1 onion, peeled and finely chopped**
- **1 celery stick, trimmed and finely sliced**
- **3 garlic cloves, peeled and crushed**
- **2 bay leaves, fresh if possible**
- **225 g/8 oz long-grain white rice**
- **475 ml/16 fl oz chicken or ham stock**

Caribbean Pork

There is a big tradition of street food in the Caribbean, and many delicious dishes, such as this recipe, can be enjoyed by tourists as they wander through the colourful streets.

Cut the pork fillet into thin strips and place in a shallow dish. Sprinkle with the ginger, chilli, garlic and 1 tablespoon of the parsley. Blend together the orange juice, soy sauce and 1 tablespoon of the oil, then pour over the pork. Cover and chill in the refrigerator for 30 minutes, stirring occasionally. Remove the pork strips with a slotted spoon and reserve the marinade.

Heat the wok over a medium heat until hot, then add the remaining oil and heat until just beginning to smoke. Stir-fry the pork for 3–4 minutes. Add the onion courgette and pepper strips, and cook for 2 minutes. Add the reserved marinade to the wok and stir-fry for a further 2 minutes.

Peel the mango and remove the stone. Cut the flesh into strips, then stir it into the pork mixture. Continue to stir-fry until everything is piping hot. Garnish with the remaining parsley and serve immediately with plenty of freshly cooked rice.

INGREDIENTS   Serves 4

- **450 g/1 lb pork fillet**
- **2.5 cm/1 inch piece of fresh root ginger, peeled and grated**
- **$^1/_2$ tsp crushed dried chillies**
- **2 garlic cloves, peeled and crushed**
- **2 tbsp freshly chopped parsley**
- **150 ml/5 fl oz pint orange juice**
- **2 tbsp dark soy sauce**
- **2 tbsp vegetable oil**
- **1 large onion, peeled and sliced into wedges**
- **1 large courgette (about 225 g/8 oz), trimmed and cut into strips**
- **1 orange pepper, deseeded and cut into strips**
- **1 ripe but firm mango**
- **freshly cooked rice, to serve**

HELPFUL HINT

Pork fillet, or tenderloin, as it is sometimes known, is a very tender cut and is always boneless. It may have some sinew attached, and this should be removed with a sharp knife.

Sticky Braised Spare Ribs

This is another dish that is easily found on the many street stalls and can be enjoyed while browsing the colourful markets.

Put the spare ribs in the wok and add enough cold water to cover. Bring to the boil over a medium-high heat, skimming off any scum that rises to the surface. Cover and simmer for 30 minutes, then drain and rinse the ribs.

Rinse and dry the wok, then return the ribs to it. In a bowl, blend the fruit juice with the white wine, hot pepper sauce, tomato ketchup, honey and treacle until smooth. Stir in the spring onions, garlic and orange zest. Stir well until mixed thoroughly. Pour the mixture over the spare ribs and stir gently until the ribs are lightly coated. Place the wok over a moderate heat and bring the ribs to the boil.

Cover then simmer, stirring occasionally, for 1 hour, or until the ribs are tender and the sauce is thickened and sticky. (If the sauce reduces too quickly or begins to stick, add a little water a tablespoon at a time until the ribs are tender.) Adjust the seasoning to taste, then transfer the ribs to a serving plate and garnish with spring onion tassels and lemon wedges. Serve immediately.

INGREDIENTS   Serves 4

- **900 g/2 lb meaty pork spare ribs, cut crossways into 7.5 cm/3 inch pieces**
- **125 ml/4 fl oz mango juice or orange juice**
- **50 ml/2 fl oz dry white wine**
- **1–2 tbsp hot pepper sauce**
- **3 tbsp tomato ketchup**
- **2 tbsp clear honey**
- **1 tbsp black treacle**
- **3 or 4 spring onions, trimmed and chopped, plus extra, cut into tassels, to garnish**
- **2 garlic cloves, peeled and crushed**
- **grated zest of 1 small orange**
- **salt and freshly ground black pepper**
- **lemon wedges, to garnish**

HELPFUL HINT

It's probably best to get your butcher to cut the ribs into pieces for you, as they are quite bony. Boiling the ribs before cooking them in the sauce reduces the fat content and ensures that they are tender and more succulent.

Speedy Pork with Yellow Bean Sauce

In this dish, tastes from the Orient have been combined with the food of the Caribbean for an eclectic mix.

Remove any fat or sinew from the pork fillet, and cut into thin strips. Blend the soy sauce, chilli powder, mango juice and cornflour in a bowl and mix thoroughly. Place the meat in a glass or cermaic bowl, pour over the soy sauce mixture, cover and leave to marinate in the refrigerator for 1 hour. Drain with a slotted spoon, reserving the marinade.

Heat the wok over a medium heat until hot, then add 2 tablespoons of the oil and heat until just beginning to smoke. Stir-fry the pork with the garlic for 2 minutes, or until the meat is sealed. Remove with a slotted spoon and reserve.

Add the remaining oil to the wok and cook the carrot, beans and spring onion for about 3 minutes, until tender but still crisp. Return the pork to the wok with the reserved marinade, then pour over the yellow bean sauce. Stir-fry for a further 1–2 minutes, or until the pork is tender. Sprinkle with the chopped parsley and serve immediately with freshly cooked egg noodles.

INGREDIENTS   Serves 4

- **450 g/1 lb pork fillet**
- **2 tbsp light soy sauce**
- **1 tsp chilli powder**
- **2 tbsp mango juice**
- **2 tsp cornflour**
- **3 tbsp vegetable oil**
- **2 garlic cloves, peeled and crushed**
- **175 g/6 oz carrots, peeled and cut into matchsticks**
- **125 g/4 oz fine green beans, trimmed and halved**
- **2 spring onions, trimmed and cut into strips**
- **4 tbsp yellow bean sauce**
- **1 tbsp freshly chopped flat-leaf parsley, to garnish**
- **freshly cooked egg noodles, to serve**

HELPFUL HINT

Try replacing the beans with other vegetables – for example, 100 g/4 oz sliced okra, 300 g/10 oz fresh shredded spinach or a 200 g/7 oz can drained and rinsed red kidney beans.

Coconut Beef

Again here the influence of the Orient can be seen. Oriental ingredients of shiitake mushrooms with fresh root ginger, groundnut oil and chilli are combined with Caribbean coconut cream and chopped coriander to give a quick and easy dish that is crammed with flavour.

Heat a wok or large frying pan, add 1 tablespoon of the oil and heat until just smoking. Add the beef and cook for 5–8 minutes, turning occasionally, until browned on all sides. Using a slotted spoon, transfer the beef to a plate and keep warm.

Add the remaining oil to the wok and heat until almost smoking. Add the spring onion, chilli, garlic and ginger and cook for 1 minute, stirring occasionally. Add the mushroom and stir-fry for 3 minutes. Using a slotted spoon, transfer the mushroom mixture to a plate and keep warm.

Return the beef to the wok, pour in the coconut cream and stock. Bring to the boil and simmer for 3–4 minutes, or until the juices are slightly reduced and the beef is just tender.

Return the mushroom mixture to the wok and heat through. Stir in the coriander and season to taste with salt and pepper. Serve immediately with freshly cooked rice.

INGREDIENTS　　　Serves 4

- **450 g/1 lb beef rump or sirloin steak, trimmed and cut into thin strips**
- **2 tbsp groundnut oil**
- **2 bunches spring onions, trimmed and thickly sliced**
- **1 habañero chilli, deseeded and chopped**
- **1 garlic clove, peeled and chopped**
- **2 cm/1 inch piece of fresh root ginger, peeled and cut into matchsticks**
- **125 g/4 oz shiitake mushrooms (or closed cup if preferred, for a less Oriental feel)**
- **200 ml/7 fl oz coconut cream**
- **150 ml/¼ pint beef stock**
- **4 tbsp freshly chopped coriander**
- **salt and freshly ground black pepper**
- **freshly cooked rice, to serve**

Jamaican Jerk Chicken

There are many recipes for jerk seasoning and, although it is possible to buy it, it is far better to make your own. Once made, store in an airtight tin or jar, and keep in a cool place. Use quickly.

Put all the jerk seasoning ingredients into a glass mixing bowl and mash together until thoroughly blended.

Rinse the chicken and pat dry with absorbent kitchen paper. Make a few cuts across the skin of the chicken, then place in a shallow dish. Spoon the jerk seasoning over the chicken and leave to marinate in the refrigerator for at least 4 hours; longer if time permits. Brush the chicken with the marinade or turn over occasionally during this time.

When ready to cook preheat the oven to 190°C/375° F/ Gas Mark 5. Place the chicken on a baking tray, and brush with the marinade left in the dish. Cook in the oven for 25–30 minutes, or until the chicken is thoroughly cooked and the juices run clear when the flesh pierced with a sharp knife. Serve garnished with the coriander sprigs.

INGREDIENTS   Serves 4

For the Jerk Seasoning
- I tsp ground allspice
- I tsp ground cinnamon
- ½ tsp freshly grated nutmeg
- I tsp dried thyme
- I tsp garlic powder
- I hot chilli, such as Scotch bonnet, deseeded and finely chopped
- 2 tbsp vegetable oil
- I tbsp butter, melted
- 2 tbsp chicken stock
- I tbsp tomato purée
- 2 tbsp lime juice
- I tbsp white wine vinegar
- I–2 tsp muscovado sugar
- ½ tsp freshly ground black pepper

- 4–8 chicken portions, depending on size
- fresh coriander sprigs, to garnish

HELPFUL HINT

If preferred, remove the skin from the chicken before marinating.

Spicy Chicken Skewers with Mango Bulgur Salad

The Middle Eastern influence on the Caribbean can be seen in this tabbouleh-style bulgur wheat salad. Tabbouleh is popular in the Dominican Republic, where it is known as 'tipili'.

If using wooden skewers, soak them in cold water for at least 30 minutes before using. (This stops them from burning during grilling.)

Cut the chicken into 5 x 1 cm/2 x $^1/_2$ inch strips and place in a shallow dish. Mix together the yogurt, garlic, chilli, turmeric, lemon rind and juice. Pour over the chicken and toss to coat. Cover and leave to marinate in the refrigerator for up to 8 hours.

To make the bulgur salad, put the bulgur wheat in a bowl. Pour over enough boiling water to cover. Put a plate over the bowl. Leave to soak for 20 minutes. Whisk together the oil and lemon juice in a bowl. Add the red onion and leave to marinate for 10 minutes.

Drain the bulgur wheat and squeeze out any excess moisture in a clean tea towel. Add to the red onion with the mango, cucumber, parsley and mint. Season to taste with salt and pepper. Toss together.

Thread the chicken strips onto 8 wooden or metal skewers. Cook under a hot grill for 8 minutes. Turn and brush with the marinade, until the chicken is lightly browned and cooked through.

Spoon the bulgur salad onto individual plates. Arrange the chicken skewers on top and garnish with the sprigs of mint. Serve warm or cold.

INGREDIENTS   Serves 4

- **400 g/14 oz chicken breast fillet**
- **200 ml/7 fl oz plain low-fat yogurt**
- **1 garlic clove, peeled and crushed**
- **1 hot red chilli, deseeded and finely chopped**
- **$^1/_2$ tsp ground turmeric**
- **finely grated rind and juice of $^1/_2$ lemon**
- **sprigs of fresh mint, to garnish**

For the Bulgur Salad

- **175 g/6 oz bulgur wheat**
- **1 tsp olive oil**
- **juice of $^1/_2$ lemon**
- **$^1/_2$ red onion, finely chopped**
- **1 ripe mango, halved, stoned, peeled and chopped**
- **$^1/_4$ cucumber, finely diced**
- **2 tbsp freshly chopped parsley**
- **2 tbsp freshly shredded mint**
- **salt and finely ground black pepper**

Hot & Spicy Chicken

On the islands, chicken is the most popular meat for the Sunday roast. During the week, chicken portions are usually served in a rich sauce, such as in this mouthwatering dish.

Using a knife, remove the skin from the chicken joints. In a shallow dish, mix together the flour, paprika, salt and pepper. Coat the chicken on both sides with the flour and shake off any excess if necessary. Heat the oil over a medium heat in a large non-stick frying pan. Add the chicken and brown on both sides. Transfer to a plate and reserve.

Add the onion and red chilli to the pan, and gently cook for 5 minutes, or until the onion is soft. Stir occasionally. Stir in the cumin and oregano, and cook for a further minute. Pour in the stock and bring to the boil.

Return the chicken to the pan, cover and cook for 40 minutes. Add the green pepper and cook for a further 10 minutes, or until the chicken is cooked. Remove the chicken and pepper with a slotted spoon and keep warm in a serving dish.

Blend the cocoa powder with 1 tablespoon warm water. Stir into the sauce, then boil rapidly until the sauce has thickened and reduced by about one-third. Stir in the lime juice, honey and yogurt.

Pour the sauce over the chicken and pepper, and garnish with the lime slices, chilli and oregano. Serve immediately with the freshly cooked rice and salad leaves.

INGREDIENTS   Serves 4

- **4 chicken portions**
- **3 tbsp plain flour**
- **$^1/_2$ tsp hot paprika**
- **2 tsp sunflower oil**
- **1 small onion, peeled and chopped**
- **1 Scotch bonnet red chilli, deseeded and finely chopped**
- **$^1/_2$ tsp ground cumin**
- **$^1/_2$ tsp dried oregano**
- **300 ml/10 fl oz chicken or vegetable stock**
- **1 green pepper, deseeded and sliced**
- **2 tsp cocoa powder**
- **1 tbsp lime juice**
- **2 tsp clear honey**
- **3 tbsp low-fat Greek-style yogurt**
- **salt and freshly ground black pepper**
- **lime slices, to garnish**
- **red chilli slices, to garnish**
- **sprig of fresh oregano, to garnish**
- **freshly cooked rice, to serve**
- **green salad leaves, to serve**

Chicken Pie with Sweet Potato Topping

The Caribbean cultivates a wide range of crops, from pineapples, mango and papaya, to cassava, yams and sweet potatoes. This recipe takes full advantage of the sweet potato. Both the white and yellow variety are grown, so use whichever you prefer and is available.

Cook both lots of potatoes in lightly salted boiling water until tender. Drain well, then return to the saucepan and mash until smooth and creamy, gradually adding the milk, then the butter, sugar and orange zest. Season to taste with salt and pepper, and reserve.

Put the chicken in a saucepan with the onion, mushrooms, leek, wine and stock cube. Season to taste. Simmer, covered, for 15–20 minutes or until the chicken and vegetables are tender. Using a slotted spoon, transfer the chicken and vegetables to a 1.1 litre/2 pint pie dish. Add the parsley and crème fraîche to the liquid in the pan and bring to the boil. Simmer until thickened and smooth, stirring constantly. Pour over the chicken in the pie dish, mix and cool.

Preheat the oven to 190°C/ 375°F/Gas Mark 5. Spread the mashed potato over the chicken filling, and swirl the surface into decorative peaks. Bake in the oven for 35 minutes, or until the top is golden and the chicken filling is heated through. Serve immediately with the green vegetables.

INGREDIENTS　　Serves 4

- **700 g/1 1/2 lb sweet potatoes, peeled and cut into chunks**
- **250 g/9 oz potatoes, peeled and cut into chunks**
- **150 ml/5 fl oz milk**
- **25 g/1 oz butter**
- **2 tsp soft brown sugar**
- **grated zest of 1 orange**
- **4 skinless chicken breast fillets, diced**
- **1 medium onion, peeled and coarsely chopped**
- **125 g/4 oz baby mushrooms, stems trimmed**
- **2 leeks, trimmed and thickly sliced**
- **150 ml/5 fl oz dry white wine**
- **1 chicken stock cube**
- **1 tbsp freshly chopped parsley**
- **50 ml/2 fl oz crème fraîche or thick double cream**
- **salt and freshly ground black pepper**
- **fresh green vegetables, to serve**

Creamy Caribbean Chicken & Coconut Soup

The coconut palm was imported around 1549, first to Puerto Rico. Coconut quickly became an important ingredient of Caribbean cuisine.

Heat a large wok, add the oil and, when hot, add the spring onion, garlic and chilli. Stir-fry for 2 minutes, or until the onion has softened. Stir in the turmeric and cook for 1 minute.

Blend the coconut milk with the chicken stock until smooth, then pour into the wok. Add the pasta with the lemon slices and bring to the boil. Simmer, half-covered, for 10–12 minutes, or until the pasta is tender; stir occasionally.

Remove the lemon slices from the wok and add the chicken. Season to taste with salt and pepper, and simmer for 2–3 minutes, or until the chicken is heated through thoroughly. Stir in the chopped coriander and ladle into heated bowls. Garnish with the extra sprigs of coriander and serve immediately.

INGREDIENTS   Serves 4

- 175 g/6 oz cooked chicken, shredded or diced
- 6–8 spring onions, trimmed and thinly sliced
- 2 garlic cloves, peeled and finely chopped
- 1 red chilli, deseeded and finely chopped
- 2 tbsp vegetable oil
- 1 tsp ground turmeric
- 300 ml/$^1/_2$ pint coconut milk
- 900 ml/1 $^1/_2$ pints chicken stock
- 50 g/2 oz small soup pasta or spaghetti, broken into small pieces
- $^1/_2$ lemon, sliced
- 1–2 tbsp freshly chopped coriander, plus extra sprigs, to garnish
- salt and freshly ground black pepper

HELPFUL HINT

Be careful handling chillies. Either wear rubber gloves or scrub your hands thoroughly, using plenty of soap and water, after chopping. Avoid touching eyes or any other sensitive areas.

Chicken in Black Bean Sauce

Black beans, also known as salted black beans, are in fact soy beans that have been preserved by fermentation in a salt and spice mix. Here their spicy, salty flavour adds a delicious and interesting element to this dish.

Place the chicken strips in a large bowl. Mix together the soy sauce, salt, caster sugar, chilli oil, 2–3 teaspoons hot pepper sauce and the cornflour. Pour over the chicken.

Heat the wok over a high heat, add the sunflower oil and, when very hot, add the chicken strips and stir-fry for 2 minutes. Add the green pepper and stir-fry for a further 2 minutes. Next add the ginger, garlic, shallot, sliced spring onion and black beans, and continue to stir-fry for another 2 minutes.

Add 4 tablespoons of the stock and stir-fry for 1 minute, then pour in the remaining stock and bring to the boil. Reduce the heat and simmer the sauce for 3–4 minutes, or until the chicken is cooked and the sauce has thickened slightly. Garnish with the shredded spring onion and serve immediately with the egg noodles.

INGREDIENTS   Serves 4

- **450 g/1 lb skinless, chicken breast fillets, cut into strips**
- **1 tbsp light soy sauce**
- **2 tbsp dry sherry or rum**
- **a little salt**
- **1 tsp caster sugar**
- **1 tsp chilli-flavoured oil**
- **2–3 tsp hot pepper sauce, plus extra to taste**
- **2 tsp cornflour**
- **2 tbsp sunflower oil**
- **2 green peppers, deseeded and diced**
- **1 tbsp freshly grated root ginger**
- **2 garlic cloves, peeled and roughly chopped**
- **2 shallots, peeled and finely chopped**
- **4 spring onions, trimmed and finely sliced, plus extra, shredded, to granish**
- **3 tbsp salted black beans, chopped**
- **150 ml/5 fl oz pint chicken stock**
- **freshly cooked egg noodles, to serve**

Duck & Exotic Fruit Stir-Fry

Marinating foods is an excellent way of adding flavour. This dish is quick and easy to prepare and cook, and makes an ideal mid-week supper dish.

Place the duck strips in a shallow bowl. Mix together the hot pepper sauce, soy sauce and chilli-flavoured oil. Pour over the duck and marinate for 2 hours in the refrigerator. Stir occasionally during marinating. Remove the duck from the marinade.

Heat the wok, add the groundnut oil and, when hot, stir-fry the marinated duck strips for 4 minutes. Remove from the wok and reserve.

Add the celery to the wok and stir-fry for 2 minutes, then add the pineapple, mango and lychees, and stir-fry for a further 3 minutes. Return the duck to the wok.

Mix together the chicken stock, tomato purée, mango chutney, wine vinegar and brown sugar. Add to the wok, bring to the boil and simmer, stirring, for 2 minutes. Serve immediately with the freshly steamed rice.

INGREDIENTS   Serves 4

- **4 duck breast fillets, skinned removed and cut into strips**
- **1 tbsp hot pepper sauce**
- **2 tbsp light soy sauce**
- **1 tbsp chilli-flavoured oil**
- **1 tbsp groundnut oil**
- **2 celery sticks, trimmed and diced**
- **1 small fresh pineapple, peeled and cut into chunks, or 225 g/ 8 oz can pineapple chunks, drained**
- **1 mango, peeled, stoned and cut into chunks**
- **125 g/4 oz lychees, peeled if fresh, stoned and halved**
- **125 ml/4 fl oz chicken stock**
- **2 tbsp tomato purée**
- **2 tbsp mango chutney**
- **2 tsp wine vinegar**
- **pinch of soft brown sugar**
- **steamed rice, to serve**

HELPFUL HINT

The exotic fruit in this recipe not only looks beautiful, but also helps to cut through the richness of the duck meat. Do not overcook the duck or it will become dry.

Spicy Chicken & Pasta Salad

A simple way to check whether a pineapple is ripe enough to use is to pull out 1 or 2 leaves from the plume – if they yield easily with little or no resistance you can rest assured that the pineapple is at its peak.

Bring a large pan of lightly salted water to a rolling boil. Add the pasta shells and cook according to the packet instructions, or until al dente. Drain and refresh under cold running water then drain thoroughly and place in a large serving bowl.

Meanwhile, melt the butter in a heavy-based pan, add the onion and cook for 5 minutes, or until softened. Add the curry paste and cook, stirring, for 2 minutes. Stir in the apricots and tomato purée, then cook for 1 minute. Remove from the heat and allow to cool.

Blend the mango chutney and mayonnaise together in a small bowl. Discard the plume from the pineapple. Stand on a chopping board and cut away and discard the skin. Cut the flesh into rings then cut out the central core using a sharp knife or metal cutter. Reserve any juice. Add the reserved pineapple juice to the mayonnaise mixture. Season the mayonnaise mixture to taste with salt and pepper.

Cut the pineapple slices into chunks and stir into the pasta together with the mayonnaise mixture, curry paste and cooked chicken pieces. Toss lightly together to coat the pasta. Sprinkle with the almond slivers, garnish with coriander sprigs and serve.

INGREDIENTS   Serves 6

- **450 g/1 lb pasta shells**
- **25 g/1 oz butter**
- **1 onion, peeled and chopped**
- **2 tbsp mild curry paste**
- **125 g/4 oz ready-to-eat dried apricots, chopped**
- **2 tbsp tomato purée**
- **3 tbsp mango chutney**
- **300 ml/10 fl oz mayonnaise**
- **1 ripe medium fresh pineapple**
- **salt and freshly ground black pepper**
- **450 g/1 lb skinned and boned cooked chicken, cut into bite-sized pieces**
- **25 g/1 oz flaked toasted almond slivers**
- **coriander sprigs, to garnish**

The Leeward

Antilles & Bermuda

Separated by thousands of miles, the Leeward Antilles and the Bermuda archipelago share some elements of common history and culture.

Curaçao
Bonaire
Aruba & the
Venezuelan
Archipelago

Aruba, Bonaire and Curaçao lie in the coastal waters off the Falcon region of Venezuela, and make up three of the six islands of the Netherlands Antilles (St Martin, Saba and St Eustatius are the others).

The islands owe much to a long history of association with the Netherlands, and on Curaçao there are even canals and gabled warehouses which have survived since colonization. Dutch pea soup sits alongside Caribbean fungi (cornmeal and okra balls) and Indian curries. The food of Bonaire, however, is limited by the poor quality of its soil and relative infertility. It is a stark, arid island, visited mostly for its crystal-clear seas and scuba diving, rather than for its cuisine.

On Aruba, the people have Dutch, Spanish, French, Portuguese, African, English and East Indian roots; their cuisine is understandably a complex blend of tastes, ingredients and

textures. A speciality is *rijstaffel* – a 'rice table' of many spiced dishes. The original dish was Indonesian, but was developed by Dutch plantation owners, who added more and more variations. Cheeses feature heavily on many menus, and often accompany Dutch-inspired meals that are considered by many to be too heavy for the tropics.

Further east along the Venezuelan coast, lying north of Caracas, are around 50 islands or cays – Los Roques – that are a federal dependency of Venezuela. The string of islands, or archipelago, is formed of coral and has been recognized as a national park since the 1970s. Many tourists visit to enjoy the reefs and wildlife, but only one island, El Gran Roque, is inhabited. The cuisine is a blend of Caribbean, South American and European influences.

Bermuda

Although lying far away from the Caribbean, in the Atlantic Ocean, the islands of Bermuda have noticeable Afro-Caribbean influences in their food. This overseas territory of the United Kingdom is commonly regarded as a single island, but there are around 138 islands in total, forming part of an extensive coral archipelago.

The land is relatively flat and dry, with no lakes or rivers. Bermuda was first settled in 1609, when shipwrecked sailors from Britain arrived here, on their way to Virginia. Now it supports a booming economy, thanks to a successful financial services sector and tourism. People are drawn to the islands' pink sandy beaches, astonishingly blue seas and subtropical climate.

Most of the islands' food has to be imported; rum, for example, was first brought to the regions from the Caribbean in the 1860s. Sweet potatoes and yams, so popular in Caribbean food, also feature in many dishes. The British brought their own culinary delights, including fish soups, or chowders, which are made from a clear fish stock with potatoes and vegetables, and flavoured with rum and sherry. A local condiment, called sherry peppers, is added liberally to provide spice. This unusual mixture is similar to the hot pepper sauces of the American South. It is made from 17 varieties of pepper, steeped in sherry and herbs, and was first used to mask the smell of tainted meat, a problem in the subtropical climate before the advent of refrigeration. Onions grow well on the Bermuda islands, and feature in a range of dishes, including onion soufflé, onion casserole and, of course, onion soup.

Africans were first brought to Bermuda by the British, not as slaves as in other places, but for their expertise in pearl fishing and cultivating West Indian crops. As slavery became more commonplace, however, the relationship between Britons and the Africans in Bermuda became more complex. Afro-Caribbean influences in Bermudan food are seen in rice and bean dishes, black-eyed peas and crab cakes.

Caribbean

Cooking
Desserts

There is an abundant supply of sweet, tangy and juicy tropical fruits in the Caribbean, so it is no surprise that fresh fruit features heavily in island dessert menus.

Creating these heavenly treats at home is easier than ever before, thanks to the increased availability of unusual fruits, such as guavas, papayas and mangoes. Ice cream, rice and tapioca puddings are often served with a liberal helping of fruit purée, locally produced honey, rum or nuts. Few desserts, however, evoke the spirit of Caribbean cuisine as indulgently as bananas fried in butter, sugar, rum and fruit juice. Enjoy!

Banana Cake

Caribbean bananas are mainly grown in the Windward Islands, which consist of St Lucia, Jamaica, Dominica, St Vincent and the Grenadines. They are smaller than those produced in Latin America and are grown using fewer pesticides.

Preheat the oven to 190°C/ 375°F/Gas Mark 5. Lightly oil and line the bottom of an 18 cm/7 inch deep round cake tin with greaseproof or baking paper.

Mash 2 of the bananas in a small bowl, sprinkle with the lemon juice and a heaped tablespoon of the brown sugar. Mix together lightly and reserve.

Gently heat the remaining brown sugar and butter in a small saucepan until the butter has just melted. Pour into a small bowl, and allow to cool slightly. Sift the flour and teaspoon of the cinnamon into a large bowl and make a well in the centre.

Beat the eggs into the cooled sugar mixture, then pour into the well of flour and mix thoroughly.

Gently stir in the mashed banana mixture. Pour half of the mixture into the prepared tin. Thinly slice the remaining banana and arrange over the cake mixture. Sprinkle over the walnuts, then cover with the remaining cake mixture.

Bake in the oven for 50–55 minutes, or until well risen and golden brown. Allow to cool in the tin, turn out and sprinkle with the remaining ground cinnamon and the caster sugar. Serve hot or cold with a jug of fresh cream for pouring.

INGREDIENTS
Cuts into 8 slices

- **3 ripe bananas**
- **1 tsp lemon juice**
- **150 g/5 oz soft brown sugar**
- **75 g/3 oz butter or margarine**
- **250 g/9 oz self-raising flour**
- **2 tsp ground cinnamon**
- **3 medium eggs**
- **50 g/2 oz walnuts, chopped**
- **1 tsp caster sugar**
- **fresh cream, to serve**

HELPFUL HINT

The riper the bananas used in this recipe, the better! Look out for reductions in supermarkets and fruit shops, as ripe bananas are often sold very cheaply. This cake tastes really delicious the day after it has been made – the sponge solidifies slightly, yet does not lose any moisture. Eat within 3–4 days.

Carrot Cake

With the abundant supply of sugar, tropical fruits and rum, cakes are crammed with heaps of flavour and aroma. Here the traditional carrot cake has been adapted to suit the Caribbean style of cooking.

Preheat the oven to 150°C/300°F/Gas Mark 2. Lightly oil and line the bottom of a 15 cm/6 inch deep square cake tin with greaseproof or baking paper.

Sift the flour, baking powder and bicarbonate of soda together into a large bowl. Beat the muscovado sugar and butter together until soft and creamy. Add the eggs to the butter and sugar mixture, then gradually stir in the flour mixture. Combine well.

Add the banana, carrots, walnuts and rum. Mix lightly together to give a soft dripping consistency, then pour into the prepared cake tin. Bake in the oven for 1¼ hours, or until light and springy to the touch and a skewer inserted into the centre of the cake comes out clean. Remove from the oven and allow to cool in the tin for 5 minutes before turning out on to a wire rack. Allow to cool completely, then remove and discard the lining paper.

To make the icing, beat together the cream cheese, orange zest, orange juice and vanilla essence. Sift the icing sugar and stir into the cream cheese mixture. Spread the cream cheese icing over the top of the cake and serve cut into squares.

INGREDIENTS
Cuts into 8 slices

- **200 g/7 oz plain flour**
- **½ tsp ground cinnamon**
- **½ tsp freshly grated nutmeg**
- **1 tsp baking powder**
- **1 tsp bicarbonate of soda**
- **175 g/6 oz unsalted butter, softened**
- **150 g/5 oz dark muscovado sugar**
- **3 medium eggs**
- **2 ripe bananas, peeled and mashed**
- **225 g/8 oz carrots, peeled and roughly grated**
- **50 g/2 oz chopped walnuts**
- **1–2 tbsp rum**

For the Icing
- **175 g/6 oz cream cheese**
- **finely grated zest of 1 orange**
- **1 tbsp orange juice**
- **1 tsp vanilla essence**
- **125 g/4 oz icing sugar**

White Chocolate & Passion Fruit Cake

Tea-time is celebrated with delicious cakes and gâteaux. Here a light and fluffy sponge is combined with creamy white chocolate and passion fruit.

Preheat the oven to 180°C/350°F/Gas Mark 4. Lightly oil and line 2 x 20.5 cm/8 inch cake tins with greaseproof paper.

Melt 125 g/4 oz white chocolate in a heatproof bowl set over a saucepan of simmering water. Stir in 125 ml/4 fl oz warm water and stir. Leave to cool.

Whisk the butter and sugar together until light and fluffy. Add the eggs, one at a time, beating well after each addition. Beat in the chocolate mixture, soured cream and sifted flours. Divide the mixture into 8 portions. Spread 1 portion into each of the tins. Bake in the oven for 10 minutes, or until firm, then turn out onto wire racks. Repeat with the remaining mixture to make 8 cake layers.

To make the icing, put 125 ml/4 fl oz water and 50 g/2 oz of the sugar in a saucepan. Heat gently, stirring, until the sugar has dissolved. Bring to the boil and simmer for 2 minutes. Remove from the heat and cool, then add 2 tablespoons of the passion fruit juice. Reserve.

Blend the remaining sugar with 50 ml/2 fl oz water in a small saucepan and stir constantly over a low heat, without boiling, until the sugar has dissolved. Remove from the heat and cool. Stir in the remaining passion fruit juice and the pulp. Cool, then strain. Using an electric whisk, beat the butter in a bowl until very pale. Gradually beat in the syrup.

Place 1 layer of cake on a serving plate. Brush with the syrup and spread with a thin layer of icing. Repeat with the remaining cake, syrup and icing, ending with a final layer of icing on top. Press the grated chocolate into the top and sides.

INGREDIENTS

Cuts into 8–10 slices

- **125 g/4 oz white chocolate, plus 125 g/4 oz extra, coarsely grated, to decorate**
- **125 g/4 oz butter**
- **225 g/8 oz caster sugar**
- **2 medium eggs**
- **125 ml/4 fl oz soured cream**
- **200 g/7 oz plain flour, sifted**
- **75 g/3 oz self-raising flour, sifted**

For the Icing
- **200 g/7 oz caster sugar**
- **4 tbsp passion fruit juice (about 8–10 passion fruit, sieved)**
- **1 1/2 tbsp passion fruit pulp**
- **250 g/9 oz unsalted butter**

HELPFUL HINT

Passion fruit is available from large supermarkets. It adds a sweet–sour flavour that goes particularly well with white chocolate.

Caribbean Rum Cake

You can vary the dried fruits in this delicious cake according to seasonal availability and personal preference.

Preheat the oven to 180°C/350°F/Gas Mark 4. Lightly oil and line a 20.5 cm/8 inch deep cake tin with greaseproof or baking paper. Place the dried fruits for the cake in a bowl. Warm the rum, then pour over the fruits and leave to marinate for at least 1 hour; longer if time permits.

Cream the butter, sugar and spices until light and fluffy. Gradually add the eggs, beating well and adding a spoonful of flour after each addition. When all the eggs have been added, stir in the remaining flour. Add the soaked dried fruit and rum. Stir together to give a soft dropping consistency. Spoon into the prepared cake tin and level the top. Mix the coconut and ground almonds for the topping together and sprinkle over the top.

Bake in the oven for 20 minutes, then arrange the fruits for the topping attractively on top. Continue to bake for a further 1 hour 20 minutes, or until a skewer inserted into the centre comes out clean. Cover the top of the cake with foil about 20 minutes after arranging the fruits on top.

Meanwhile, put the 50g/2oz sugar in a heavy-based saucepan with the 4 tablespoons rum. Heat gently until the sugar has dissolved, then bring to the boil and continue to boil steadily for 2–3 minutes until a light syrup is formed. Reserve.

Once the cake is cooked, warm the syrup slightly, then slowly pour over the cake. Allow to cool in the tin before turning out and discarding the lining paper. This cake is best if left for 2–3 days before cutting. Store in an airtight tin.

INGREDIENTS
Cuts into 12 slices

- **100 g/4 oz ready-to-eat dried papaya, finely chopped**
- **100 g/4 oz ready-to-eat dried pineapple, finely chopped**
- **100 g/4 oz ready-to-eat dried mango, finely chopped**
- **225 g/8 oz sultanas**
- **225 g/8 oz raisins**
- **8 tbsp rum**
- **225 g/8 oz unsalted butter or margarine, softened**
- **225 g/ 8 oz light muscovado sugar**
- **1 tsp ground cinnamon**
- **1 tsp ground allspice**
- **½ tsp freshly grated nutmeg**
- **4 medium eggs, beaten**
- **300 g/10 oz self-raising flour**

For the Topping
- **2–3 tbsp shredded coconut**
- **2 tbsp ground almonds**
- **350 g/12 oz ready-to-eat dried fruits, cut into chunks**
- **50 g/2 oz sugar**
- **4 tbsp rum**

Orange Freeze

These delicious fruity filled orange shells are the perfect way to chill out when the heat of the day hits.

Set the freezer to rapid-freeze. Using a sharp knife, carefully cut the lid off each orange. Scoop out the flesh from the orange, discarding any pips and thick pith. Place the shells and lids in the freezer, and chop any remaining orange flesh. Purée the mango flesh until smooth, then whisk together the orange juice, orange flesh and vanilla ice cream until well blended. Pour into a shallow flat container.

Cover and freeze for about 2 hours, occasionally breaking up the ice crystals with a fork or a whisk. Stir the mixture from around the edge of the container into the centre, then level and return to the freezer. Do this 2 or 3 times, then leave until almost frozen solid.

Place a large scoop of the ice cream mixture into the frozen orange shells. Add another scoop on top, so that there is plenty outside of the orange shell, and return to the freezer for 1 hour. Arrange the lids on top and freeze for a further 2 hours, until the filled orange shell is completely frozen solid.

Meanwhile, using a nylon sieve, press the raspberries into a bowl using the back of a spoon and mix together with the icing sugar. Spoon the raspberry coulis onto 4 serving plates and place an orange at the centre of each one. Dust with extra icing sugar and serve decorated with the redcurrants. Remember to return the freezer to its normal setting.

INGREDIENTS   Serves 4

- **4 large oranges**
- **1 small ripe mango, peeled, stoned and chopped**
- **about 300 ml/10 fl oz low-fat vanilla ice cream**
- **225 g/8 oz raspberries**
- **75 g/3 oz icing sugar, sifted, plus extra for dusting**
- **redcurrant sprigs, to decorate**

HELPFUL HINT

The fresh citrus in this dish works to clear the palate. The acidity combines well with the creaminess of the ice cream. Lemons would also work well in this recipe.

Mango Sorbet

Mangoes have over the years become increasingly popular. Grown in tropical climes, they are at their best when eaten ripe – slightly underripe fruits are not juicy, so for maximum flavour make sure that your fruits are ripe.

Turn the freezer to rapid-freeze at least 1 hour before freezing. Peel the mango and cut in half on either side of the stone. Dice into small pieces. Blend in a food processor to form a smooth purée. Squeeze the limes and add to the processor, then blend for 1 minute. Scrape the purée into a bowl.

Put the sugar and 150 ml/5 fl oz water in a heavy-based saucepan and heat gently until the sugar has dissolved. Bring to the boil and boil steadily for 5 minutes, or until a light syrup is formed. Cool slightly, then stir into the mango purée.

Whisk the egg whites until soft peaks are formed, then stir into the mango mixture. Pour into a freezable container and freeze for 1 hour.

Stir the mango mixture to break up any ice crystals. Return to the freezer and freeze for a further 1 hour. Repeat the stirring and freezing once more, then leave in the freezer for 2 hours, or until frozen. Serve in scoops.

INGREDIENTS   Serves 4

- **2 large ripe mangoes**
- **2 or 3 limes (to give 3–4 tbsp juice)**
- **50 g/2 oz granulated sugar**
- **2 medium egg whites**

HELPFUL HINT

Remember to return the freezer to its original setting. An ice-cream maker can be used if preferred; this will give a slightly different texture and look. Follow the manufacturer's instructions.

Tipsy Tropical Fruit

Malibu is one of the most well known and popular Caribbean drinks. It is a sweet coconut-flavoured white rum with hints of almond and mocha, which is perfect to use both in desserts and in cocktails.

Drain the pineapple chunks, reserving the juice. Pat the pineapple dry on absorbent kitchen paper. Peel the guavas and cut into wedges. Halve the papaya and scoop out the black seeds. Peel and cut into 2.5 cm/1 inch chunks. Halve the passion fruit and scoop out the pulp into a small bowl.

Heat the butter in a wok, add the pineapple and stir-fry over a high heat for 30 seconds. Reduce the heat and add the guava and papaya. Drizzle over the orange juice and cook for 2 minutes, stirring occasionally, taking care not to break up the fruit.

Using a slotted spoon, remove the fruit from the wok, leaving any juices behind, and transfer to a warmed serving dish. Add the creamed coconut to the wok with the sugar and reserved pineapple juice. Simmer for 2–3 minutes, stirring until the coconut has melted.

Add the Malibu or white rum to the wok and heat through, then pour over the fruit. Spoon the passion fruit pulp on top and serve hot with spoonfuls of ice cream, decorated with a sprig of mint.

INGREDIENTS   Serves 4

- **225 g/8 oz can pineapple chunks in natural juice**
- **2 guavas**
- **1 papaya**
- **2 passion fruit**
- **25 g/1 oz unsalted butter**
- **1 tbsp orange juice**
- **50 g/2 oz creamed coconut, chopped**
- **50 g/2 oz soft light brown sugar**
- **2 tbsp Malibu liqueur or white rum**
- **sprigs of fresh mint, to decorate**
- **vanilla ice cream, to serve**

HELPFUL HINT

Passion fruit are small, round, purplish fruits which are ripe when the skin is dimpled and wrinkled.
To use them, it is necessary to slice them across the middle and scoop out the seeds and flesh.
The seeds are edible and have a lot of flavour, but can be sieved out if preferred.

Caramelized Oranges in an Iced Bowl

This stunning iced bowl makes a sensational serving dish for fruit desserts. It is very simple to make and can be kept in the freezer and used for a number of occasions.

Set the freezer to rapid-freeze. Place a few ice cubes in the base of a 1.7 litre/3 pint freezable glass bowl. Place a 900 ml /1½ pint glass bowl on top of the ice cubes. Arrange the flower heads and fruits in between the 2 bowls, wedging in position with the ice cubes.

Weigh down the smaller bowl with some heavy weights, then carefully pour cold water between the 2 bowls making sure that the flowers and the fruit are covered. Freeze for at least 6 hours, or until the ice is frozen solid.

When ready, remove the weights and, using a hot damp cloth, rub the inside of the smaller bowl until it loosens sufficiently to remove. Place the larger bowl in a sink half-filled with very hot water. Leave for about 30 seconds, or until the ice loosens. Do not to leave in the water for too long or the ice will melt. Remove the bowl and leave in the refrigerator. Return the freezer to its normal setting.

Thinly pare the zest from 2 of the oranges, then cut into matchsticks. Using a sharp knife, cut away the zest and pith from all the oranges, catching the juices in a bowl. Slice the oranges, discarding pips, and re-form each into its original shape. Secure with cocktail sticks, then place in a bowl.

Heat 300 ml/10 fl oz water with the orange zest and sugar in a pan. Stir until the sugar has dissolved. Bring to the boil. Boil for 15 minutes until a caramel colour. Remove the pan from the heat. Stir in the liqueur and pour over the oranges. Allow to cool. Chill for 3 hours, turning the oranges occasionally. Spoon into the ice bowl and serve.

INGREDIENTS   Serves 4

For the Ice Bowl
- **about 36 ice cubes**
- **fresh flowers and fruits**

- **8 medium-sized oranges**
- **225 g/8 oz caster sugar**
- **4 tbsp Grand Marnier or Cointreau**

HELPFUL HINT

This iced bowl can hold any dessert. Why not fill with flavoured ice creams?

Caribbean Spiced Rice Pudding

This is a deliciously spicy rice pudding that is crammed full of tropical dried fruits – perfect comfort food for all ages.

Heat the soft brown sugar and butter in a heavy-based saucepan until blended, stirring throughout. Add the rice and allspice. Cook, stirring, for 2 minutes.

Slowly pour the milk into the rice mixture and pour in the coconut milk, then add the cinnamon stick. Bring to the boil, reduce the heat to a gentle simmer and cook, stirring occasionally, for 20 minutes, or until the rice is tender. Add more milk if it is becoming too dry and reduce the heat a little more.

Cut the mango away from the central stone, then peel. Chop the flesh into small pieces. If using fresh pineapple discard the plume, skin and central core from the pineapple, and cut the flesh into small pieces.

Add the sultanas to the rice pudding and cook for 2 minutes, then add the mango, pineapple and mandarin. Heat for 1–2 minutes, or until hot, remove the cinnamon stick (if it hasn't broken up) , then serve warm.

INGREDIENTS   Serves 4

- **50 g/2 oz soft brown sugar**
- **25 g/1 oz unsalted butter**
- **100 g/4 oz white basmati rice**
- **1 tsp ground allspice**
- **300 ml/10 fl oz milk**
- **300 ml/10 fl oz coconut milk**
- **1 cinnamon stick, bruised**
- **1 ripe mango**
- **½ medium pineapple or 200g/7 oz can pineapple pieces, drained**
- **100 g/4 oz sultanas**
- **2 fresh mandarins, peeled and segmented**

HELPFUL HINT

If preferred, all milk can be used rather than half milk and half coconut milk.

For extra special occasions, stir in 2–3 tablespoons rum.

Fried Bananas with Sugar and Rum

Choose bananas that are ripe but still slightly firm. Overripe fruit will collapse during cooking and even though the finished dessert will still taste delicious the appearance will be spoilt.

Heat the butter and sugar in a frying pan over a gentle heat until melted, stirring frequently. Add the allspice and lime zest and juice to the pan with the rum. Heat, stirring occasionally, for 1–2 minutes, or until blended.

Peel the bananas, then add to the frying pan and cook for 2–3 minutes, or until softened and turning golden. Carefully turn the bananas over halfway through the cooking time.

Arrange the bananas on individual plates, pour over a little of the sauce and serve with vanilla ice cream, decorated with lime wedges.

INGREDIENTS   Serves 4

- **75 g/3 oz unsalted butter**
- **50 g /2 oz caster sugar**
- **½ tsp ground allspice**
- **grated zest and juice of 1 lime**
- **6–8 tbsp rum**
- **4 ripe but firm bananas**
- **vanilla ice cream, to serve**
- **lime wedges, to decorate**

HELPFUL HINT

For a more alcoholic pudding, add 2–3 tablespoons rum at the end after cooking the bananas, heat for 1 minute, then carefully ignite. Draw off the heat and allow the flames to subside before serving.

Index

Dishes with full recipes are shown in *italic* type.